Multi-Engine Pilot Manual

JEPPESEN
SANDERSON

JS314127A

INTRODUCTION

The *Multi-Engine Pilot Manual* is a comprehensive textbook reference designed for private or commercial pilots who wish to add multi-engine ratings to their pilot certificates. The manual and other materials are designed for applicants training under FAR Part 141 in FAA approved schools, as well as those training under FAR Part 61 who are not affiliated with an approved school. The course also will benefit rated multi-engine pilots who wish to update their skills with refresher training or to complete their biennial flight reviews.

The manual is divided into three parts and contains textbook narrative, workbook exercises, and pilot briefings. The textbook section is divided into three chapters, which represent logical divisions of multi-engine subject areas. Corresponding workbook exercises allow the applicant to check his progress in the academic phase of the course. At strategic points in the course, pilot briefings provide the basis for in-depth discussions with the instructor, covering multi-engine operations, procedures, and maneuvers.

The manual is supplemented with several other comprehensive study materials.

1. Multi-Engine Pilot Audiovisual Presentations review and reinforce the concepts presented in the Multi-Engine Manual. These motivating visual aids present essential subjects in brilliant color and synchronized sound.
2. Multi-Engine Stage and Final Examinations are designed to evaluate the applicant's progress throughout the course. The examinations are required items for a multi-engine course conducted under FAR Part 141 in an FAA approved school.
3. The *Multi-Engine Pilot Training Syllabus* provides a lesson-by-lesson guide for completion of the ground and flight training required under FAR Part 141. The Training Syllabus is required for all applicants who are enrolled in approved schools and also is beneficial for applicants seeking certification outside of approved schools.

The information presented in the Multi-Engine Course provides the necessary framework for a successful multi-engine training program. Applicants who complete this course of study under the guidance of a qualified instructor will be well prepared for the FAA Multi-Engine Flight Test.

TABLE OF CONTENTS

PART I—TEXT

PART II—WORKBOOK

PART III—PILOT BRIEFINGS

chapter 1

MULTI-ENGINE OPERATIONS AND SYSTEMS

INTRODUCTION

The transition to the multi-engine airplane is exciting for most pilots, regardless of background experience. Suddenly they are exposed to an airplane with dramatically increased performance capabilities, compared to most single-engine airplanes. To derive the greatest benefit from multi-engine training, it is important that the applicant familiarize himself with the distinctive features of multi-engine flight.

The first section of this chapter provides the framework for transition to the multi-engine airplane under normal operating conditions. It introduces the concepts and considerations which are distinctive to multi-engine flight, such as aerodynamics, takeoff planning, flight profile, and maneuvers.

The second section of the chapter provides a comprehensive treatment of systems generally found on twin-engine airplanes. A broad knowledge of systems is an essential element of multi-engine training. The subjects covered in this chapter include propeller, fuel, fuel injection, electrical, landing gear, turbocharging, ice control, and cabin heating systems.

SECTION A—PROCEDURES AND MANEUVERS

This section serves to accentuate the operational differences between multi-engine and single-engine airplanes. It begins with a discussion of twin-engine aerodynamics, defines important terms and concepts, and considers the necessary sequence of preflight planning. Following this is a description of the entire multi-engine flight profile with a concluding analysis of typical maneuvers used during multi-engine flight training.

Generally, this section is limited to normal two-engine operations; however, an understanding of many "single-engine" terms and concepts is required even for normal operations. Consequently, single-engine considerations are presented when necessary for better clarification. For example, an understanding of the single-engine service ceiling and the accelerate-stop distance is necessary for normal takeoff planning.

MULTI-ENGINE AERODYNAMICS

The principles of aerodynamics governing the flight of single-engine airplanes also apply to those with more than one engine. Multi-engine airplanes respond to the four forces of flight just as any other airplane, regardless of the number of powerplants. The primary aerodynamic differences between single-engine and multi-engine flight result from the location of the engines.

Figure 1-1 illustrates that thrust in conventional multi-engine airplanes is not directed along the centerline, as it is in airplanes with one engine. Conventional twin-engine airplanes have one engine mounted on each wing, producing thrust *parallel* to the longitudinal axis. Therefore, the thrust vectors are displaced from the airplane's centerline.

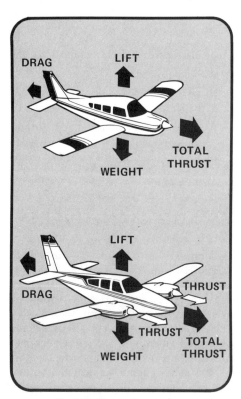

Fig. 1-1. Thrust Comparison

INDUCED AIRFLOW

The most important advantage of wing-mounted engines is that a substantial amount of lift is derived from propeller slipstream. This *induced airflow* also occurs in single-engine airplanes; however, it is not as effective or apparent in aircraft where the powerplant is mounted along the centerline. Figure 1-2 illustrates the effect of induced airflow.

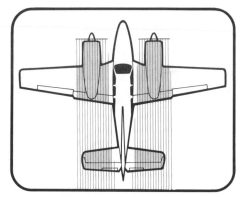

Fig. 1-2. Induced Airflow

The lift provided by induced flow is an important consideration during landing and in imminent stall recoveries. A sharp power reduction will cause an instantaneous loss of propeller slipstream flow and a corresponding loss of total lift. This could result in a high sink rate or stall if power is reduced suddenly during a slow final approach. On the other hand, rapid addition of power when an imminent stall has been identified could prevent further stall development. However, induced flow should never be relied on as the sole factor in stall recovery. The addition of power in combination with other normal stall recovery procedures should be utilized.

TURNING TENDENCIES

In single-engine airplanes, left-turning tendencies are caused by both asymmetrical propeller loading (P-factor) and torque. Multi-engine airplanes have an even greater tendency to turn during climbs or other high angle of attack

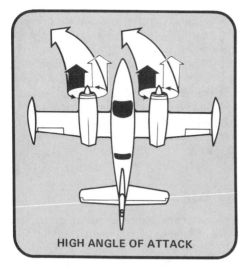

HIGH ANGLE OF ATTACK

Fig. 1-3. Asymmetrical Propeller Loading

maneuvers due to the additional engine and propeller. The position of these engines in relation to the airplane center-line allows asymmetrical thrust to exert a more forceful turning moment, as shown in figure 1-3. In addition, the effects of torque also are greater in multi-engine airplanes because of the more powerful engines usually encountered. Torque is caused by the tendency of the airplane itself to turn about the propeller and engine crankshaft. It acts in the direction opposite propeller rotation, as shown in figure 1-4. In twins

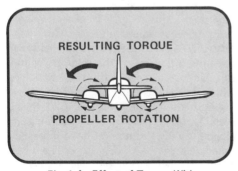

RESULTING TORQUE

PROPELLER ROTATION

Fig. 1-4. Effect of Torque With Conventional Engines

equipped with counterrotating engines, however, the effect of torque is elim-inated. The torque from one engine cancels the effect of the other, as shown in figure 1-5.

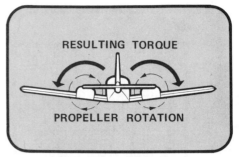

RESULTING TORQUE

PROPELLER ROTATION

Fig. 1-5. Effect of Torque With Counterrotating Engines

MULTI-ENGINE CEILINGS

The maximum operating altitudes of airplanes in use today are as varied as the aircraft themselves. Some turbocharged light twins are designed to operate as high as 30,000 feet, while normally aspirated models are limited to altitudes between 15,000 and 20,000 feet under gross weight conditions.

Normally aspirated engines lose power progressively as the airplane ascends be-cause of decreasing atmospheric pres-sure. This gradual loss of power deter-mines the maximum altitude capabilities of the airplane. Contrary to popular belief, climb performance is based on excess power and not on the creation of additional lift. The amount of lift pro-duced during a climb is nearly the same as the amount required for level flight.

Turbocharging increases the operating altitudes considerably over normally aspirated engines. It provides sea level or greater manifold pressure at high alti-tudes where normally aspirated engines can only provide manifold pressure equal to the ambient atmospheric pressure. However, once the airplane has climbed to the turbocharger's critical altitude, the engines begin to progressively lose power with altitude. From that point, turbocharged engines progressively lose power like their normally aspirated counterparts.

SERVICE CEILING

The *service ceiling* is defined as the maximum density altitude where the

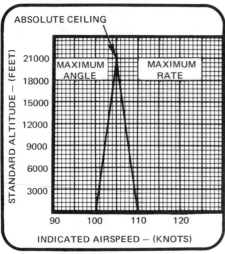

Fig. 1-6. Absolute Ceiling

best rate-of-climb airspeed will produce a 100 f.p.m. climb at gross weight in the clean configuration with both engines producing maximum continuous power. The *single-engine* service ceiling refers to the altitude at which the rate of climb is 50 f.p.m. with one engine inoperative.

ABSOLUTE CEILING

The *absolute ceiling* is defined as the maximum density altitude the airplane is capable of attaining or maintaining at gross weight, in the clean configuration, and at maximum continuous power. The absolute ceiling is closely related to the best angle-of-climb and best rate-of-climb speeds. Figure 1-6 shows that, as altitude increases, the best angle-of-climb speed increases, while the best rate-of-climb speed decreases. The point where the two speeds converge is the absolute ceiling of the airplane.

MULTI-ENGINE V-SPEEDS

The chart in figure 1-7 lists the critical airspeeds (V-speeds) normally encountered in multi-engine flying. The manufacturer's operating instructions should be consulted for other speeds, such as the operating range for landing gear and wing flaps.

PREFLIGHT PREPARATION

Preflight planning must include a careful analysis of the factors governing the

takeoff, climb, cruise, and landing phases of flight. The pilot of a multi-engine airplane must not only be concerned with these normal preflight planning considerations, but he also must consider and plan his course of action in the event of an engine failure. Since the takeoff and climb to a safe altitude make up the most critical phase of flight, a large percentage of preflight activity involves takeoff planning.

TAKEOFF PLANNING

The first consideration during accurate preflight planning is the determination of density altitude. Besides calculating its effect on the takeoff ground run and airplane performance, the pilot should compare *density altitude* with the *single-engine service ceiling* of the airplane. The combination of high airport elevations and high temperatures often results in a takeoff density altitude that is above the airplane's single-engine service ceiling. Under these conditions, the probability of a sustained climb to a safe circling altitude after an engine failure is very remote. In this situation, a rejected takeoff or a controlled descent to a forced landing may be the only alternatives.

The second consideration in takeoff planning is the analysis of the airplane's runway requirement under existing conditions. This requirement includes both the determination of the takeoff ground run and the accelerate-stop distance, which is the distance required to accelerate the airplane to a specified speed (usually liftoff speed) and, assuming an engine failure occurs at precisely that speed, return to a full stop. The pilot should be aware that the accelerate-stop distance under some conditions may be nearly *double* the normal ground run. As an example, the pilot may determine that a 6,000-foot runway is adequate after calculating that a distance of 3,400 feet is required for the takeoff ground run. However, further calculations may indicate that the accelerate-stop distance

MULTI-ENGINE OPERATIONS AND SYSTEMS

Designation	Description	Airplane Configuration or Significance of Speed	A/S Ind. Marking
V_{SO}	Stalling Speed—Landing Configuration	Engines zero thrust, propellers takeoff position, landing gear extended, flaps in landing position, cowl flaps closed	Low speed end of white arc
V_{S1}	Stalling Speed—Specified Configuration	Engines zero thrust, propellers takeoff position, landing gear and flaps retracted	Low speed end of green arc
V_{MC} (V_{MCA})	Minimum Control Airspeed (Air Minimum Control Speed)	Takeoff or maximum available power on operating engine, critical engine windmilling (or feathered if auto feather device is installed), landing gear retracted, flaps in takeoff position	Red radial line *
V_{SSE}	Intentional One Engine Inoperative Speed	Minimum speed for intentionally rendering one engine inoperative in flight for pilot training	
V_X	Best Angle-of-Climb Speed	Speed which produces most altitude gain over a given distance with both engines operating; obstruction clearance speed	
V_Y	Best Rate-of-Climb Speed	Speed which produces most altitude gain in a given time with both engines operating	
V_{XSE}	Best Angle-of-Climb Speed (Single Engine)	Speed which produces most altitude gain over a given distance with one engine inoperative	
V_{YSE}	Best Rate-of-Climb Speed (Single Engine)	Speed which produces most altitude gain in a given time with one engine inoperative	Blue radial line *
V_{LE}	Maximum Landing Gear Extended Speed	Maximum speed for safe flight with landing gear extended	
V_{FE}	Maximum Flap Extended Speed	Maximum speed with wing flaps in a prescribed extended position	High speed end of white arc
V_A	Design Maneuvering Speed	Speed below which structural damage will not occur as a result of full control deflection	
V_{NO}	Maximum Structural Cruising Speed	Maximum speed for normal operation	High speed end of green arc
V_{NE}	Never-Exceed Speed	Maximum design speed without structural failure	Red Line

* Aircraft receiving type certificates under FAR Part 23 after November 11, 1965, will have these markings.

Fig. 1-7. Multi-Engine V-Speeds

is 6,500 feet, which, in fact, makes the total safety of the takeoff questionable. Therefore, it becomes apparent that the accelerate-stop distance is a primary limiting factor when evaluating airplane performance versus available runway.

The distance required to clear obstacles should include not only the twin-engine performance standards, but also those for single-engine performance. In addition, the pilot must consider rising terrain and distant obstructions which could not be cleared when considering the anticipated single-engine rate of climb. It is not uncommon, particularly

when the density altitude and single-engine service ceiling are nearly the same, to find that the terrain rises more rapidly than the single-engine climb rate. In this situation, the probability of a single-engine climb to a safe circling altitude becomes improbable.

In addition, complete takeoff planning should include the determination of available alternatives. These can include suitable areas for forced landings, nearby alternate airports, and the decision to takeoff with reduced fuel and/or baggage to increase single-engine performance. Finally, the pilot should review the engine-out airspeeds and procedures just prior to each takeoff. This procedure makes each speed available for instant recall and completes the pretakeoff planning. The most critical engine-out airspeed is V_{MC}. This is discussed in greater detail in Chapter 3.

Note:

The FAA abbreviation V_{MC} is used throughout this manual; however, some manufacturers may prefer V_{MCA} in reference to this critical speed.

CLIMB PLANNING

When operating under normal conditions, a *cruise climb* is usually appropriate. A cruise climb produces a slower rate of climb, but is advantageous in that it decreases total trip time, allows better forward visibility, provides better engine cooling, and increases passenger comfort. However, if it is necessary to climb at a faster rate to reach favorable winds aloft or better weather conditions, the best rate-of-climb airspeed (V_Y) can be used throughout the climb. Most airplane manufacturers provide performance charts to reflect the elapsed time, fuel consumption, and distance required for climb to various altitudes.

An additional climb consideration is use of the best angle-of-climb airspeed (V_X). This airspeed should be used only to clear obstructions immediately after takeoff. A sustained climb at V_X results in an increase in the total trip time because of slower groundspeed. Long climbs at V_X also decrease engine cooling because of the high angle of attack and reduced airflow. In addition, performance charts usually *are not* available to determine the rate of climb produced by sustained climbs at V_X.

ENROUTE PLANNING

Enroute planning should include selection of the cruising altitude and an appropriate power setting. With this information, the airplane performance charts can be used to determine the true airspeed, range, and the enroute fuel consumption. The fuel consumption should be determined carefully to allow an adequate reserve in the event the flight cannot be completed as originally planned and diversion to an alternate airport is required.

Planning should also include consideration of the terrain, particularly in mountainous areas. This is particularly important when the flight is conducted at altitudes in excess of the single-engine service ceiling. In the remote event that single-engine flight becomes necessary at high altitudes, the pilot should plan a course of action during the gradual descent to the single-engine service ceiling. He should be familiar with the areas of lower terrain and the availability of alternate airports along the route of flight.

MULTI-ENGINE OPERATIONS

USE OF CHECKLISTS

Regardless of whether a pilot flies a single-engine or a multi-engine airplane, he must be aware of the importance of using a printed checklist for each airplane he flies. Checklists supplied by the manufacturer can be used effectively with the addition of minor revisions for optional equipment installation. However, most flight schools and instructors prefer to use their own checklists which are compiled from experience, show more detail, and, generally, are better suited to the training situation. The most efficient use of any checklist is attained by reading each item aloud and actually touching that item to insure that it is operating normally and/or is positioned properly.

PREFLIGHT INSPECTION

A thorough preflight inspection is recommended prior to departure. The pilot's operating handbook or flight school checklist should be consulted so that important items are not overlooked. Inspection procedures during intermediate stops are normally limited to a check of the flight control hinges, fuel and oil quantity, and security of fuel and oil filler ports. However, if the airplane has been operated from marginal airports or in adverse weather conditions, a more extensive check should be performed. In addition, the pilot should inspect the airplane thoroughly after extended storage, when major maintenance has been performed, or after it has been exposed to extensive ground handling in crowded hangars.

Once the preflight inspection is complete, the airplane is ready for boarding. The seats should be adjusted, seatbelts fastened, and the cabin door secured. If necessary, the passenger briefing should be completed. Then, the pilot can devote his full attention to engine starting procedures.

ENGINE STARTING

Prior to starting any engine, the pilot should make a careful visual check of the area to insure that it is clear and that the resulting propeller blast will not endanger people or property on the ramp. During engine starting at night, it may be advisable to turn the rotating beacon on momentarily to alert anyone in the area of the impending engine start. The position lights must be on for any night operations, including engine starts.

The airplane checklist usually contains starting procedures which are appropriate to the existing conditions. Normal, cold weather, hot start, and flooded engine procedures are provided. The checklist also may designate which engine is to be started first. This determination is normally a result of the position of the battery in relation to the engines. For example, if the battery is located in the left wing, the left engine should be started first. This employs shorter battery cables and causes less energy loss to the left engine than the right. Airplanes that have the battery installed in the nose, cabin floorboards, or tail section generally do not specify which engine is to be started first.

TAXIING

During taxi, the pilot has three methods of directional control—the steerable nosewheel, differential braking, and differential power. For nearly all situations, nosewheel steering provides adequate maneuverability to taxi safely. However, if it is necessary to make tight turns at slow taxi speeds, differential power can be used. For example, to make a tight turn to the left, the power on the left engine is reduced and the power on the right engine is increased. At the same time, left rudder is applied. Figure 1-8 shows that the radius of turn depends on the amount of differential power applied.

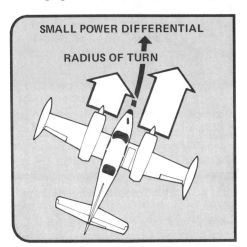
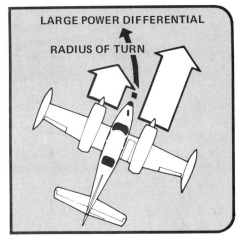

Fig. 1-8. Differential Power for Turns

Prior to taxiing the airplane, the brakes should be checked for proper operation. This check is most safely accomplished by applying a *small* amount of power to both engines to start the airplane moving, then reducing the power and applying the brakes. If any brake malfunction is noted, the airplane should not be taxied or flown until the problem is corrected.

The least desirable method of directional control is differential braking. This technique increases the wear on both the tires and brakes and can easily result in

brake overheating and subsequent failure.

CROSSWIND TAXI

Increased directional control during crosswind taxiing also can be accomplished by the use of differential power. As shown in figure 1-9, when additional power is applied to the upwind engine, a turning vector away from the wind is created. The velocity of the crosswind component determines the amount of differential that is required. However, if the crosswind velocity is quite high, the steerable nosewheel must be used to assist in directional control. Otherwise,

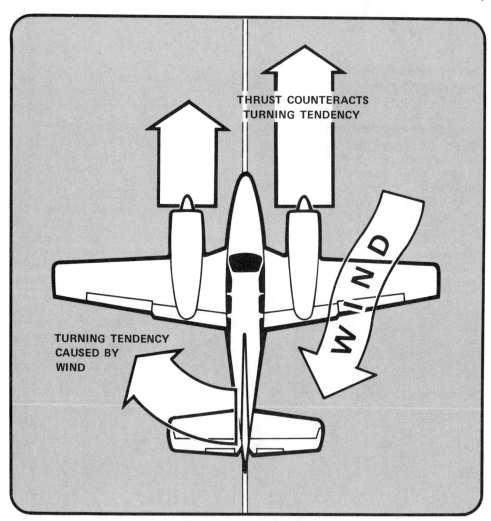

Fig. 1-9. Crosswind Taxi

high power on the upwind engine will result in excessive taxi speed and the need for frequent braking.

PRETAKEOFF CHECK

Prior to takeoff, each airplane system is given a thorough functional inspection. Most of the items on the checklist are familiar to the pilot who has flown high performance single-engine airplanes, with the exception of the propeller feathering checks. Generally, multi-engine airplanes are equipped with full feathering propellers, which allow propeller rotation to be stopped in the event of an engine failure in flight. The check is performed by moving the propeller control lever to the full aft position and noting the change in engine r.p.m. If the propeller governor is operating properly, the r.p.m. should decrease rapidly as the propeller begins to feather. Then, the lever is moved full forward immediately to prevent the propeller blades from feathering. If the r.p.m. changes slowly or erratically, the feathering mechanism is not operating properly and in-flight feathering may not be possible. In this situation, flight should not be attempted before an authorized mechanic inspects and repairs the propeller system. A complete analysis of the propeller system is included in Section B of this chapter.

TAKEOFF

When the pretakeoff checklist is completed, the airplane is taxied onto the active runway and aligned carefully with the runway centerline. It is a good operating practice to bring the airplane to a complete stop on the runway prior to power application. As the power is advanced smoothly, the pilot should be alert for uneven thrust, signs of engine roughness, or sluggish engine acceleration. When takeoff power is attained, the engine instruments should be checked to determine that both engines are operating properly. This check should include the manifold pressure, r.p.m., fuel flow, and oil pressure/temperature. If

any instrument indicates an abnormal system operation, the takeoff should be discontinued. The airspeed indicator also should be checked early in the takeoff run, since it is essential for safe flight in the event of engine failure.

During a normal takeoff, the airplane is allowed to accelerate to the manufacturer's recommended rotation and liftoff speed. Generally, this speed will be approximately V_{MC} plus five knots. Under no conditions should the airplane become airborne at a speed less than the minimum single-engine control speed (V_{MC}). After liftoff, the airplane is accelerated to the two-engine best rate-of-climb airspeed (V_Y) and this speed is maintained until a safe maneuvering altitude is reached. V_Y is used for this portion of the climb because it provides an adequate rate of climb and the speed normally is equal to or higher than the single-engine best rate-of-climb airspeed (V_{YSE}). Therefore, if an engine failure occurs, the airplane has already attained the airspeed which will produce the best single-engine climb performance.

Once the airplane is well clear of the runway, a positive rate of climb is established, and insufficient runway remains for landing, the landing gear should be retracted. It is recommended that prior to retracting the landing gear, the brakes be applied momentarily to stop the rotation of the main wheels. Centrifugal force caused by the rapidly rotating wheels expands the diameter of the tires and, if ice or mud has accumulated in the wheelwells, the rotating wheels may rub as they enter.

The first power reduction should not take place until the landing gear is fully retracted and the airplane is at a safe maneuvering altitude. Once these two requirements are met, the power is reduced to the climb setting by decreasing the manifold pressure first, then the propeller r.p.m. When the climb power setting is established, the fuel pump for

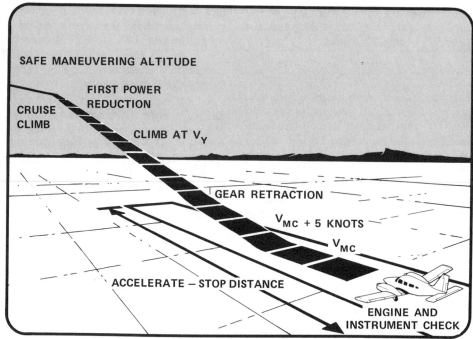

Fig. 1-10. Takeoff and Climb Profile

each engine is turned off *individually* and each mixture is adjusted for climb. The fuel pumps are not turned off simultaneously for safety reasons. Since an engine failure is more likely to occur during changes in power or fuel flow, one pump is turned off and the engine operation is monitored before the second pump is turned off. The same procedure is used when leaning the mixtures or changing fuel tanks. The complete takeoff and climb profile is illustrated in figure 1-10.

CROSSWIND TAKEOFF

Crosswind takeoffs in a multi-engine airplane require the same basic technique as that used in a single-engine airplane. Specifically, the upwind aileron is used to prevent side drift and rudder is used for directional control. As with other takeoffs, ground contact is maintained until the recommended liftoff speed is attained. Once the airplane is airborne, a crab is established to maintain the desired ground track. The landing gear is retracted when a positive rate of climb is

established and a landing is no longer possible on the remaining runway.

SHORT-FIELD TAKEOFF AND MAXIMUM CLIMB

The short-field takeoff and maximum climb may be divided into three separate phases—the takeoff ground run and lift-off, the first segment of climb, and the second segment of climb. To begin the first phase of the maneuver, the airplane is taxied into position at the end of the runway, the flaps extended (if required by the airplane manufacturer), the brakes applied, and full power applied to both engines. After the engines are developing full power, the brakes are released to begin the takeoff ground run.

As the airplane accelerates, the elevator control is maintained in the neutral position to create the least amount of aerodynamic drag. Then, elevator back pressure is applied to raise the nosewheel smoothly so the airplane breaks ground at the airspeed specified in the pilot's operating handbook. This airspeed is

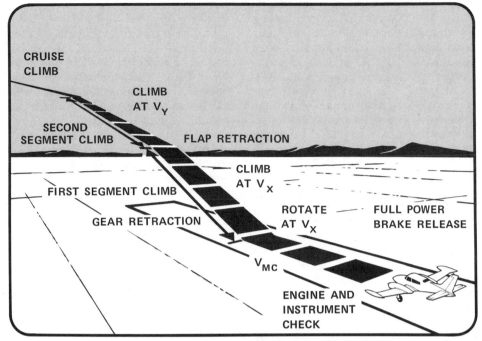

Fig. 1-11. Short-Field Takeoff and Maximum Climb Profile

normally the two-engine best angle-of-climb airspeed (V_X). If V_X is less than V_{MC}, a climb at no less than V_{MC} is recommended.

After the airplane breaks ground and a positive climb rate is established, the gear is retracted and V_X, or V_{MC}, whichever is higher, is maintained until all obstacles are cleared. Then, the flaps are retracted and the airplane is allowed to accelerate to the best rate-of-climb airspeed. During the second segment of the climb, the airspeed is maintained at V_Y. When a safe maneuvering altitude is reached, the power is reduced and a cruise climb established, if desired. Figure 1-11 illustrates the takeoff procedure and associated airspeed utilization.

TAKEOFF CONSIDERATIONS

Every takeoff, regardless of the type, involves a very important consideration which results in safe multi-engine operations. Specifically, every takeoff must be planned and executed with the anticipation of an engine failure. If this habit pattern is established early in flight

training and the situation does occur, the pilot will be prepared to perform the necessary procedures smoothly, accurately, and without hesitation.

CLIMB

When a fast rate of climb is not required, passenger comfort should be considered. Multi-engine airplanes generally have performance capabilities which produce a rate of climb in excess of 1,000 f.p.m. However, this high climb rate may result in considerable ear discomfort to the pilot and passengers. Therefore, an airspeed should be selected to produce a lower climb rate, such as 500 f.p.m. This technique results in added comfort, plus reduced trip time due to the higher airspeed used for climb.

When operating an airplane equipped with normally aspirated engines, climbs to high altitudes will require periodic increases in throttle settings to maintain a constant percent of power. Once the full throttle setting is reached, the percent of available horsepower will decrease, along with the aircraft's performance. When operating at altitudes in excess of 5,000 feet MSL, the mixtures are leaned periodically to maintain smooth engine operation and maximum performance. If the airplane is turbocharged, 75 percent power normally is maintained throughout all or most of the climb. If 75 percent power is used, the mixture is adjusted to the climb fuel-flow setting until cruising altitude and power are established.

During climb operations, all of the engine instruments are monitored and maintained within the normal operating ranges. In particular, the cylinder head temperature is important due to the reduced airflow during the climb. The proper temperature range normally can be maintained by adjusting the cowl flaps (if appropriate). If cylinder head temperatures become excessive, the airplane may be leveled off momentarily or a higher climb speed may be selected. Additional procedures for combating high cylinder head temperatures include enriching the mixtures and increasing engine r.p.m.

PROPELLER SYNCHRONIZATION

The propellers should be synchronized after the initial power reduction during the climb. If they are not rotating at the same r.p.m., an annoying, pulsating sound will be created within the cabin. As the difference in r.p.m. increases, the pulsation will increase. To synchronize the propellers, the pilot matches the r.p.m. indications on the tachometers, then slowly retards one propeller control and notes whether the sound increases or decreases. If the pulsation increases, the control lever is moved in the opposite direction until the pulsating sound stops. When the sound is eliminated, the propellers are synchronized.

CRUISE

As the desired cruising altitude is reached, the airplane pitch attitude is reduced for level flight, the power setting adjusted, and the excess control

pressures trimmed. After the airplane stabilizes in level flight, the mixture controls are adjusted to provide the best fuel-air ratio and, therefore, the best rate of fuel consumption for the power setting selected. The pilot's operating handbook should be consulted to determine the recommended fuel flow for the existing altitude and outside air temperature. Another method of adjusting the mixture is use of the exhaust gas temperature (EGT) gauge, which measures the temperature of the exhaust gases at the exhaust manifold. This method of adjusting the fuel-air mixture is the most accurate. The entire system is described in Section B of this chapter.

DESCENT

The higher airspeeds and altitudes commonly used for flight in multi-engine airplanes generally require a planned descent profile for passenger comfort and satisfactory operation of such systems as turbocharging and cabin pressurization. Maintenance of normal engine temperatures also limits the rate of descent.

The following conditions can be used as an example of proper descent planning.

Cruising altitude . . . 11,500 ft. MSL
Pattern altitude . . . . . .2,100 ft. MSL
Descent rate . . . . 500 f.p.m.
Descent groundspeed . . . . . 155 kts.

The descent problem is solved by using the following steps.

1. Determine the required altitude loss of 9,400 feet by subtracting 2,100 feet from 11,500 feet.
2. Calculate the descent time by dividing 9,400 feet by 500 f.p.m., resulting in 18.8 minutes for the descent. (Round this to 19 minutes.)
3. Finally, use the flight computer to determine the distance required for the descent by finding the distance traveled in 19 minutes at a speed of 155 knots. This calculation indicates that 49 n.m. (57 s.m.) will be

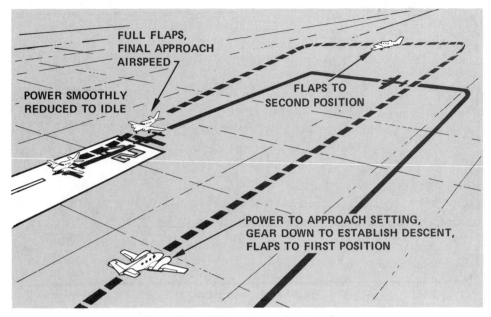

FULL FLAPS,
FINAL APPROACH
AIRSPEED

POWER SMOOTHLY
REDUCED TO IDLE

FLAPS TO
SECOND POSITION

POWER TO APPROACH SETTING,
GEAR DOWN TO ESTABLISH DESCENT,
FLAPS TO FIRST POSITION

Fig. 1-12. Stabilized Approach to Landing

required. From these calculations, determine that a 500 f.p.m. descent should be initiated 49 n.m. from the destination to arrive at the airport at the proper altitude.

In most instances, the descent is accomplished at or slightly above the cruising airspeed, but not above the maximum speed of the normal operating range. In this manner, groundspeed is not sacrificed during the descent. As the airplane descends, the mixture controls are enriched as necessary for smooth engine operation. As the destination airport is approached, the checklist is reviewed in preparation for the landing.

LANDING

Figure 1-12 illustrates a typical traffic pattern used by most light and medium twin-engine airplanes. Although each make and model has slight procedural variances, the fundamentals of the traffic pattern and landing procedures are the same.

If the descent has been planned properly, the airplane should arrive at the traffic pattern altitude just before entering the downwind leg. At that time, the power setting is adjusted to reduce the airspeed to the desired traffic pattern speed. When the airplane is established on the downwind leg, the landing check is performed. If the landing gear is extended at approximately mid-field, the increased drag further decelerates the airplane so that the first increment of flaps may be extended with little or no change in the power setting.

As the aircraft continues throughout the base leg and final approach, additional flaps are extended to control the airspeed and descent rate. On final approach the pilot should verify that the propeller controls are positioned at high r.p.m. and the mixtures are set for the appropriate altitude. Ideally, the power is reduced gradually as the airplane approaches touchdown in the proper landing attitude. After touchdown, directional control is maintained through the combined use of rudder and nosewheel steering. The brakes are used, as necessary, to slow the aircraft and the

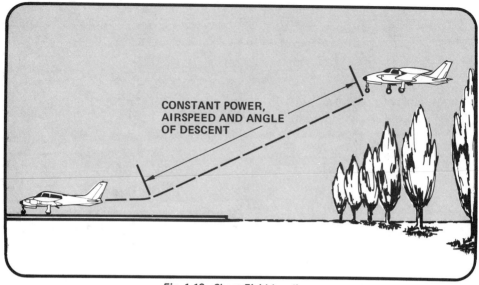

CONSTANT POWER, AIRSPEED AND ANGLE OF DESCENT

Fig. 1-13. Short-Field Landing

flaps may be raised to increase braking efficiency.

Crosswind landings are made using either the crab method, the wing-low method, or a combination of the two. Any crab used is removed with downwind rudder just prior to touchdown in a near three-point attitude. When landing in strong crosswinds, the minimum flaps necessary for the runway length are used.

SHORT-FIELD APPROACH AND LANDING

The short-field approach and landing procedure involves maneuvering the airplane over a 50-foot obstacle to a landing using the shortest possible roll-out distance. The approach and landing are performed with full flaps to achieve a slower approach speed and steeper descent angle.

The downwind and base leg portions of the short-field landing traffic pattern are the same as those used for a normal landing. The difference between the two procedures is found on the final approach in that a slightly higher approach is planned to clear the obstacle. The final approach is planned so that full flaps are extended, a constant airspeed is estab-

lished, and a constant angle of descent is used throughout the approach. The power should remain nearly constant until the landing flare, where the throttles are closed smoothly, resulting in a landing with little or no floating. After landing, the flaps are retracted, elevator back pressure is maintained, and braking applied as necessary. Figure 1-13 illustrates the short-field final approach and landing technique.

REJECTED LANDING

When executing a rejected landing (go-around), the pilot normally applies full throttle, since the propeller and mixture controls were positioned on final for a possible go-around. The next step is to reduce drag as much as possible and initiate a climb. The flaps are retracted to the takeoff position and then the landing gear is retracted. Since the power application and flap retraction may cause a large trim change, the pilot should trim the aircraft, as necessary. After all obstacles are cleared, any remaining flaps are retracted and the power is reduced, as necessary. After the aircraft has been restabilized and retrimmed, the landing checklist is reviewed.

MULTI-ENGINE FLIGHT MANEUVERS

STEEP POWER TURNS

Steep turns are performed with a minimum bank angle of 50°. These turns should not be performed at speeds in excess of maneuvering speed due to the high load factors that may be induced.

The control pressures required to maintain bank angle and altitude are greater than those required in a single-engine airplane. Small pitch changes will result in greater altitude variations because of the higher airspeeds involved and the greater amount of excess power available. Therefore, special attention is directed to smooth and coordinated control usage, including trim. Each of the flight instruments is monitored for precise references and outside visual cues are checked for any indication of a deviation from the proper pitch attitude. Corrections are made promptly before any large correction is needed to maintain the desired altitude and bank angle.

FLIGHT AT MINIMUM CONTROLLABLE AIRSPEED

Flight at minimum controllable airspeed is conducted with both engines operating and at an airspeed sufficiently slow that any further increase in angle of attack or load factor will result in a stall. This is accomplished in both cruise and landing configurations.

To enter the maneuver, the power is reduced to approximately 12 to 15 inches of manifold pressure and the attitude is increased slowly as the airspeed decreases. Approximately five knots above the desired airspeed, the power is increased to stop the deceleration. If the maneuver is performed in the landing configuration, the gear and flaps are extended at the appropriate airspeeds as the airplane decelerates. Considerably more power is required to maintain altitude in the landing configuration

because of the large amount of drag. Several transitions between the cruise and landing configuration should be practiced so the maneuver can be performed at a constant altitude and heading.

To return to level flight the flaps are reduced to the takeoff position, the landing gear is retracted, and the remaining flaps are retracted as the speed increases. Throughout the transition and during the maneuver, the airplane heading and altitude must remain constant.

IMMINENT STALLS

The applicant for a multi-engine class rating is required to demonstrate recognition of and recovery from imminent stalls in the landing and cruise configurations. These stalls are performed with and without power from straight and turning flight, climbs, and glides. On no occasion is the pilot required to demonstrate a full stall or a stall with any engine throttled and the other engine developing effective power. Performance of a stall in an aircraft which is producing asymmetrical power can cause a spin or other dangerous situation.

The stalls required during a multi-engine class rating flight test are imminent stalls, rather than fully developed stalls. Generally, recovery is initiated when the airplane's tail begins to buffet.

APPROACH-TO-LANDING CONFIGURATION

To perform imminent stalls in the approach-to-landing configuration, a satisfactory altitude is selected and the area is cleared for other traffic. Then, power is reduced, gear and flaps are extended, and a wings-level glide at normal approach speed is established. After the aircraft is stabilized in the glide, the nose is raised to reduce the indicated airspeed by approximately one knot per second.

As the aircraft decelerates, there are three basic indications of an imminent stall—reduction in sound level, decreas-

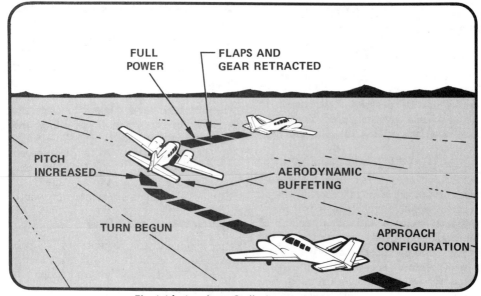

FULL POWER   FLAPS AND GEAR RETRACTED

PITCH INCREASED

AERODYNAMIC BUFFETING

TURN BEGUN

APPROACH CONFIGURATION

Fig. 1-14. Imminent Stall—Approach to Landing

ing control response, and aerodynamic buffeting. As the aircraft decelerates, there is a reduction in the tone and intensity of slipstream noise and a change in engine sounds. These changing sounds are a useful indication of an approaching stall.

As the speed of the airplane decreases and the slipstream slows, the controls become less responsive. Then, at the point that an imminent stall is reached, a slight aerodynamic buffet is felt. As soon as this buffet begins, the angle of attack is decreased smoothly, full power added, and flaps and gear retracted. As best angle-of-climb airspeed is reached, the nose is raised gently and a climb is established. Figure 1-14 illustrates the procedure used to perform an imminent stall in the approach configuration.

If the stall is practiced in the landing configuration, it is important to use the proper recovery sequence to break the stall and reduce drag so the aircraft will accelerate quickly to the proper speed. There are four steps in this sequence.

1. Reduce angle of attack.
2. Apply full power.
3. Raise flaps to the takeoff setting.
4. Retract the landing gear after a positive rate of climb is established.

TAKEOFF-AND-DEPARTURE CONFIGURATION

To perform imminent stalls in the takeoff-and-departure configuration, a safe altitude is selected and the area is cleared for other traffic. Then, a maximum performance departure is simulated, because this type of stall is most likely to occur during the initial climb over an obstacle.

To simulate the departure, the aircraft is decelerated to best angle-of-climb speed with the flaps in the takeoff setting and the landing gear retracted. As best angle-of-climb speed is approached, power is established and back pressure is increased to simulate the departure. After the climb is established, the pitch attitude is increased smoothly to a position that will cause the aircraft to stall.

As this attitude is maintained, the decreasing sound level and reduced control response give progressive indications of the approaching stall. At the first aerodynamic indication of a stall (as the buffeting begins), the nose is lowered smoothly and full power applied. The aircraft is then allowed to accelerate to best angle-of-climb speed and the climb is resumed.

ACCELERATED MANEUVER STALLS

The term "accelerated" is not related to the rapidity with which a stall is induced. Instead, it refers to a stall which occurs at a higher-than-normal airspeed because of an increased load factor. Normally, a steep turn is used to increase the load factor and induce an accelerated stall.

To enter the stall, the aircraft is slowed to 1.25 times the stall speed in the landing configuration. This is done to simulate the approach speed and configuration used in the traffic pattern. Then, the airplane is rolled smoothly into a bank of approximately 45°. As the bank is being established, back pressure is increased gradually to induce the stall.

During accelerated stall practice, the decreasing sound level and progressively sluggish control response associated with other stalls do not occur to the same degree. This is due to the fact that the aircraft stalls at a higher speed. Therefore, the major indication of the accelerated stall is the aerodynamic buffeting. Recovery should be initiated at the first indication of the stall. The nose is lowered smoothly, wings rolled level, and full power added. Recovery is complete when straight-and-level flight is attained.

SECTION B—GENERAL SYSTEMS

The following section provides the multi-engine applicant with a general overview of representative systems incorporated on modern twin-engine airplanes. This section is *not* designed to be used in lieu of the specific pilot's operating handbook, but, rather, to acquaint the pilot with the major systems and system variations found in general aviation airplanes. *For specific operational details and limitations, the appropriate pilot's operating handbook must be consulted.*

PROPELLER SYSTEMS

The propellers installed on most multi-engine aircraft may be classified as constant speed, controllable pitch, full feathering propellers. Depending on the propeller manufacturer, there are two types of controlling mechanisms. The first utilizes boosted engine oil pressure and nitrogen pressure within the propeller hub. The second system uses boosted engine oil pressure and mechanical springs for system operation.

CONSTANT SPEED PROPELLERS

When a fixed pitch propeller system is installed on an aircraft, the propeller r.p.m. changes according to the speed and angle of attack of the airplane. For example, if the airplane begins to accelerate, the propeller r.p.m. tends to increase. Conversely, if the airspeed decreases, as in a climb, the propeller r.p.m. decreases. The constant speed system eliminates propeller r.p.m. fluctuation by changing the *blade angle* automatically according to the conditions. If the airspeed increases, the blade angle increases; conversely, when the airplane decelerates, the blade angle decreases automatically. Maintenance of a constant r.p.m. by variation of the propeller blade angle also tends to maintain the desired propeller angle of attack and optimum propeller efficiency. The constant speed system requires a hydraulic propeller governor and pitch change mechanism.

When the propeller control lever is adjusted to the desired r.p.m., the hydraulic governor is thereby adjusted to maintain that r.p.m. If the engine speed begins to increase above the r.p.m. for which the governor is adjusted, the governor actuates the pitch-change mechanism in the propeller hub and the blade angle increases. When the blade angle increases, the angle of attack is increased, resulting in higher drag loading. The increased load causes a lower propeller speed. As the engine r.p.m. decreases, the governor reverses the process in the pitch-change mechanism, which returns the blade angle to the original pitch and the engine to the desired speed. When the engine speed begins to decrease below the selected r.p.m., the process is the same, except the blade angle is decreased.

PROPELLER CONTROLS

The propeller control levers allow the pilot to select the desired r.p.m., which the constant speed system will then maintain. To select the desired setting, the controls are moved either forward or aft. If the controls are moved full forward, the blade angle is decreased and high r.p.m. results. When the controls are moved aft, the governor increases the blade angle and the r.p.m. decreases. If the propeller control levers are moved to the full aft position into the feather detents, the blade angle is increased to nearly align with the relative wind. This action stops the rotation of the propeller, as shown in figure 1-15.

Fig. 1-15. Propeller in Full Feather

The purpose of the full feathering propeller is to eliminate the parasite drag developed by a windmilling propeller. When the propeller is windmilling, the drag is increased greatly and airplane performance is decreased significantly. This consideration becomes critical during engine-out operations.

FEATHERING

Since the propellers on multi-engine airplanes are not only constant speed but also full feathering, two mechanisms are required to change the blade angle from low pitch to full feather. The basic pitch-change mechanism depends on boosted engine oil pressure from the propeller governors. However, if the pitch-change mechanism depended entirely on oil pressure to feather the propeller, the loss of oil pressure or governor failure would prevent the propeller from being feathered. Therefore, a secondary method of increasing blade angle is required for full feathering pitch-change mechanisms.

When the propeller is spinning, the normal aerodynamic twisting forces are acting on the propeller to move it towards low pitch (high r.p.m.). These forces can be altered by changing the blade's center of mass in lieu of opposing oil pressure from the propeller governor. To alter the center of mass, featherable propellers have counterweights attached to the base of each blade, as shown in figure 1-16. As the propeller rotates, the counterweight's center of mass moves toward the blade's plane of rotation, tending to increase the blade angle, as shown in figure 1-17. The centrifugal force produced by the counterweights is designed to be slightly *greater* than the aerodynamic twisting force, and hydraulic pressure is used to aid the aerodynamic force in decreasing the blade angle. In addition to the counterweights, the propeller system incorporates either compressed air or a mechanical spring to aid in moving the blades to the full feather position.

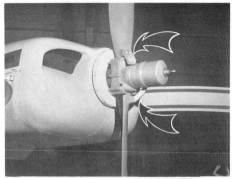

Fig. 1-16. Propeller Counterweights

An important aspect of the feathering procedure is engine speed. A locking device in the propeller hub prevents feathering the propeller at lower engine speeds, usually below 700 to 800 r.p.m. This insures that the propeller does not feather during engine starting or shutdown, when the engine oil pressure is very low. The pilot's operating handbook should be consulted for specific operational details.

POWER APPLICATION OR REDUCTION

Correct propeller operation is directly related to proper engine care. In flight, it is very important to maintain the manifold pressure and propeller r.p.m. within their respective operating ranges. For specific limitations and guidelines, the appropriate pilot's operating handbook should be consulted.

Proper propeller operation is critical during the phases of flight requiring power application or reduction. Because the propellers are constant speed, the basic operating procedures must be followed. Specifically, for power application, the propeller control levers must be advanced first, followed by increases in manifold pressure. For power reduction, the manifold pressure must be reduced prior to reduction in propeller r.p.m. This procedure maintains the proper balance between internal cylinder pressure and the power required of the engine.

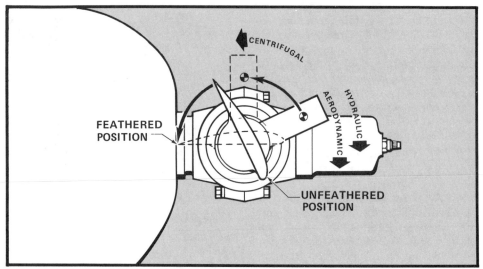

Fig. 1-17. Effect of Counterweights

PROPELLER SYNCHRONIZING SYSTEM

Propeller synchronizing systems are installed on some multi-engine airplanes to match the r.p.m. of the two engines automatically. The system operates on the principle that the left engine is *slaved* to the right engine. Therefore, the left engine follows any change in r.p.m. of the right engine. This type of system aids in elimination of propeller vibration and noise within the cabin.

System operation is simple in that the pilot first sets the desired r.p.m. of both propellers, insuring that the two propellers are within 50 r.p.m. of each other. When the propeller synchronizer switch is activated, the propeller r.p.m. of the left engine will follow changes in r.p.m. of the right engine over a *limited range* of engine speeds. This limited range prevents the left engine from losing more than 50 propeller r.p.m. in the event the right engine is feathered with the synchronizer system activated. The limitation placed upon the use of the system is that it must be deenergized during takeoffs, landings, and single-engine operation.

AUTOFEATHER SYSTEM

Autofeather systems are installed on some high performance turboprop twin-engine airplanes to feather the propeller automatically in the event of a power loss during takeoff. The system is armed for operation prior to takeoff and turned off during the climb when a safe altitude is reached.

The autofeather system is an electrically energized system using microswitches in the power levers and a power sensing switch within the engine system. As the power levers are advanced for takeoff, the microswitches are activated and the system is *armed* for operation. In the event either engine loses power during the takeoff ground run, rotation, or early phases of climb, the power sensing switch senses the power loss. At that time, the autofeather system causes a drop in oil pressure from the propeller governor and the propeller on the failed engine feathers automatically. Once the propeller has been feathered by the autofeather system, the pilot must be cautious *not* to retard the power lever on the failed engine until the system has been deenergized. If the power lever is retarded, the microswitch is opened.

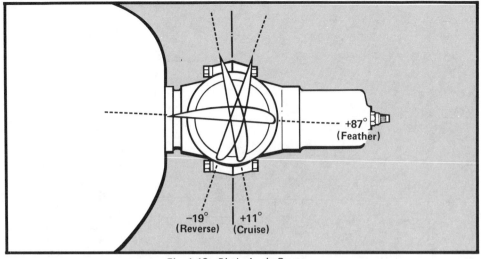

Fig. 1-18. Blade Angle Range

This deactivates the system and the propeller may unfeather. Therefore, when a propeller feathers, the autofeather should be deenergized and normal engine shutdown procedures followed.

REVERSIBLE PROPELLER SYSTEM

As an additional system feature of turboprop powered twin-engine airplanes, reversible propellers are installed to decrease the landing roll. A reversible propeller does not reverse in direction of rotation, but merely changes blade angle into the *negative* blade angle range. For example, the *total range* of a particular propeller may be +87° to -19° blade angle. The blade angle for feather would be +87°, while the cruise blade angle may be +11° to +17°. The taxi blade angle may be +9°, zero thrust may be +2° and the reverse range may be 0° to -19°. This concept is shown in figure 1-18.

The propeller that has reversing capability simply uses a negative blade angle in conjunction with engine power to create reverse thrust. The negative blade angle is created by increasing the oil pressure in the propeller hub to force the blades to a negative angle of attack. The increase in oil pressure occurs when the power levers are moved into the reverse range, which signals the propeller governor to increase oil pressure. Each power lever controls its respective engine and reversing capability.

FUEL SYSTEMS

The fuel systems installed on most general aviation multi-engine airplanes are designed for simplicity and ease of operation. Although each individual airplane system may have operational and structural differences, all fuel systems have the same basic components.

The fuel system may be described as two independent systems, one installed in each wing, which permit each engine to operate from its own fuel supply. The two systems are interconnected by crossfeed lines which allow the distribution of fuel from one tank to the opposite engine, if necessary. The following paragraphs present a discussion of common fuel system components.

SYSTEM COMPONENTS

FUEL TANKS

The fuel cells, or fuel tanks, generally are located within each wing, outboard of

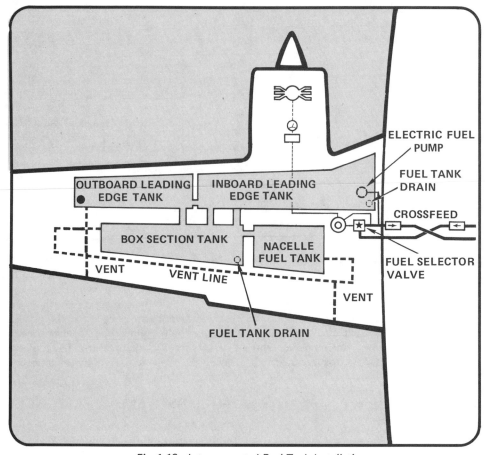

Fig. 1-19. Interconnected Fuel Tank Installation

the engine. Some models of airplanes utilize a multi-tank installation where as many as four tanks are incorporated internally within each wing. These tanks generally have one filler port and are interconnected to provide a single source of fuel for the respective engine. This installation is shown in figure 1-19.

Some types of airplanes, however, utilize individual tank installations which are designated as the *main tank* and *auxiliary tank*. These fuel tanks may be installed internally at different locations within the wing or externally on the wingtips. Generally, they have individual filler ports and are not interconnected. Therefore, each tank provides an indivi-

dual fuel supply to the engines, as shown in figure 1-20.

FUEL PUMPS

The fuel system of any multi-engine airplane incorporates two types of pumps to provide fuel pressure to the engine. The first type is a mechanical engine-driven pump installed on each engine. The second type is an electric boost pump which is operated by a simple switch located on the control panel. There are two electric pumps (one for each engine) installed within the fuel system. Their locations vary between makes and models of airplanes.

Engine-Driven Fuel Pumps

One engine-driven fuel pump is installed on each engine upstream from the fuel

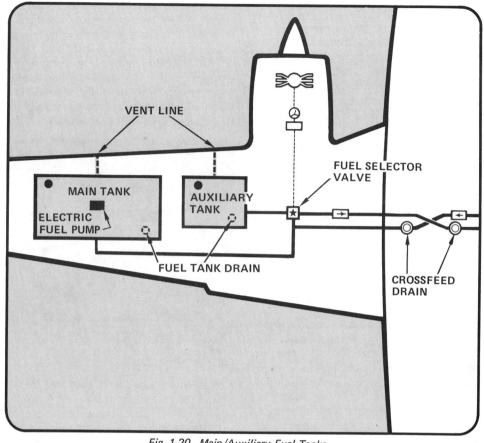

Fig. 1-20. Main/Auxiliary Fuel Tanks

injection unit. The pump draws fuel from the tanks and forces it through the injector unit. Since this type of pump is mechanically actuated, it is dependent upon operation of the engine. Therefore, during the engine start procedure, the electric boost pump must be activated to provide fuel to the engine. After the engine is running smoothly, the electric pump is turned off and the mechanical pump should provide adequate fuel pressure.

Electric Fuel Pumps

Electric fuel pumps are installed for two purposes—to provide fuel pressure during engine start and to provide fuel pressure in the event a mechanical pump should fail or malfunction. Therefore, most systems require the electric pump to be in operation during periods when an engine-driven pump failure could be critical. Such situations include takeoffs, landings, and maneuvering at slow airspeeds and/or low altitudes.

The locations of the electric pumps within the fuel system vary according to the airplane manufacturer, but two basic locations are typically used. The first type is installed within the engine nacelle upstream from the mechanical pump. The second type is located within each main fuel tank, submerged in the fuel. Although these pumps are located in different positions within the system, both are capable of providing adequate fuel pressure to sustain nearly maximum engine power in the event of a mechanical pump failure.

Operational Check

The engine starting procedure provides a check of both the electric pump and the mechanical pump for proper operation. During the engine start, the electric pump should provide fuel flow and pressure with the fuel selector on and the mixture control full rich.

The engine-driven mechanical pump may be checked by simply turning off the electric pump after the engine is running smoothly. If the mechanical pump is inoperative, the engine will fail due to insufficient fuel pressure. The combination of the two pumps is critical to safety, and flight must not be attempted when either pump is malfunctioning.

FUEL SELECTOR CONTROL

The fuel selector controls are located inside the cabin and may vary in appearance and operation, depending on the airplane manufacturer. The fuel selector control shown in figure 1-21 is a three-position selector which allows the pilot to select either on, off, or crossfeed for each engine. With this type of system, fuel can be transferred from one side of the airplane to the engine on the opposite side. Therefore, all of the fuel is considered to be available for crossfeed operations.

Fig. 1-21. Three-Position Fuel Selector Control

Figure 1-22 depicts another type of common fuel selector control. Each control has four positions, indicating main, auxiliary, crossfeed, and off. This type of fuel selector control is utilized on airplanes that have auxiliary fuel tanks not interconnected with the main tanks. When the auxiliary tanks are selected, no fuel is used from the main tanks.

Fig. 1-22. Four-Position Fuel Selector Control

FUEL SELECTOR VALVES

Fuel selector valves have the function of routing the fuel from the appropriate tank to the engine. These valves generally are operated through a mechanical linkage from the fuel selector control inside the airplane. All fuel must pass through the fuel selector valves enroute from the tank to the engine. In the event a fuel selector valve is malfunctioning, the fuel selector control will not seat properly in the detents or the control will be difficult to move. If either of these difficulties occur, a mechanic should be consulted prior to starting the engines.

CROSSFEED SYSTEM

The crossfeed feature of any fuel system allows the pilot to direct fuel from one side of the airplane to the opposite engine. However, the individual pilot's operating handbook should be consulted for specific crossfeed system operation and limitations. As mentioned previously, the fuel from all tanks may not be available for crossfeed purposes.

Generally, the crossfeed system is utilized during emergency single-engine operations. For example, if the right engine is inoperative, the crossfeed may be used to direct fuel from the right tanks to the left engine. If extended single-engine flight becomes necessary, fuel usage from each side of the airplane should be alternated approximately every 30 minutes. In this manner, fuel will be consumed so it equalizes the weight distribution between the two sides of the airplane.

FUEL TANK VENTS

Although the fuel tank vents are a small portion of the total fuel system, they are vital to its proper operation. These vents may be located in a variety of positions, but all serve the purpose of allowing air to replace the fuel that is consumed by the engines. In addition, some types of fuel vents are exposed to ram air pressure, which creates a downward pressure on the fuel within the tank. This slight additional pressure aids the fuel pumps in delivering fuel to the engines.

In the event a fuel tank vent is blocked, a vacuum is created within the tank as the engine consumes the fuel. This condition results in engine failure due to fuel starvation. Therefore, the fuel tank vents are an important preflight inspection item and should be checked for blockage due to wax, dirt, or other foreign material. As an additional precaution, it may be recommended that extremely dusty conditions be avoided during taxi and takeoff.

FUEL STRAINERS

The fuel strainers (sometimes termed gascolators) are installed to filter and trap any accumulations of moisture or sediment in the fuel supply. One strainer is installed on each engine between the fuel selector valve and the engine-driven fuel pump. As the fuel passes through the strainer enroute to the fuel pump, the water and/or debris accumulates in the bottom of the strainer bowl, as

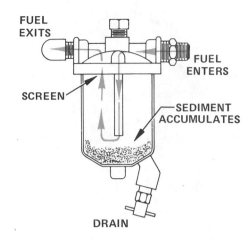

Fig. 1-23. Fuel Strainer

shown in figure 1-23. During the preflight inspection, the quick drain is opened momentarily to remove the accumulation of contaminants.

QUICK DRAINS

In addition to the quick drains located on the fuel strainers, quick drains are usually installed for each fuel tank and crossfeed line. Each drain should be opened momentarily during the preflight inspection to remove any contaminants that have settled to the bottom of the tank or fuel line. The opening of the fuel tank and fuel line quick drains should be accomplished *prior* to draining the strainers. If the strainer is drained before the fuel tanks, a portion of the fuel within the tank is moved towards the strainer. This movement disturbs the fuel and the contaminants within the tank and makes removal of the contaminants virtually impossible until they have settled back to the bottom of the tank. Therefore, the pilot should drain the outboard tank first, followed by the inboard tank, then the strainer, and finally the crossfeed lines.

FUEL SYSTEM MONITORING INSTRUMENTS

The instruments associated with most fuel systems are the fuel-pressure and fuel-flow gauges, as shown in figure 1-24.

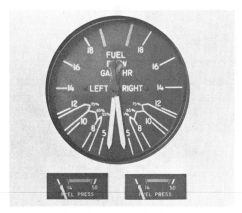

Fig. 1-24. Fuel System Monitoring Instruments

The indications of these two instruments should be monitored throughout the operation of the airplane.

Fuel-Pressure Gauge

The fuel-pressure gauge indicates fuel pressure at the injector inlet. The gauge is marked with a green arc to indicate the normal range of fuel pressure. In addition to the pressure gauge, some types of airplanes are equipped with warning lights to alert the pilot to low fuel pressure. If inadequate pressure is observed or the warning lights illuminate, the electric fuel pump should be activated, since the mechanical pump may be malfunctioning. The following list describes several conditions which can create low fuel pressure.

1. Damaged fuel selector valve
2. Fuel selector control in improper position
3. Blocked or broken fuel line
4. Blocked fuel tank vent
5. Malfunctioning fuel pump

Fuel-Flow Gauge

The fuel-flow gauge indicates fuel consumption of each engine measured in gallons per hour. The instrument measures fuel flow by sensing a pressure drop within the fuel-flow divider. When a constant pressure is supplied to the engine-driven fuel pump, the pressure downstream may be measured against the constant static pressure. The constant static pressure is available through a vent line extending from the gauge to the engine compartment, which automatically compensates the instrument for altitude. When the instrument measures the two pressures, the resultant differential pressure can be calibrated in gallons or pounds per hour of fuel flow.

FUEL INJECTION SYSTEM

Control of fuel and air entering the combustion chamber is one of the most critical factors in operating high performance engines. Extremes in fuel-air mixtures, pressures, and temperatures can greatly reduce an engine's performance, or even cause it to fail. Although float carburetion may be an adequate means of control in some cases, fuel injection provides a more accurate method of measuring and distributing the desired amount of fuel to each cylinder. The contribution of fuel injection to an engine's overall performance can be shown in terms of lower fuel consumption per unit of horsepower, increased horsepower per unit of engine weight, and lower operating temperatures.

SYSTEM COMPONENTS

Fuel injection systems are utilized on most modern multi-engine airplanes. Since each individual airplane may have slightly different operating procedures and characteristics, a careful review of the appropriate pilot's operating handbook is required prior to operating an unfamiliar system.

As shown in figure 1-25, the continuous flow fuel injection system has four basic components. The numbered callouts in the illustration correspond to the following items.

1. Engine-driven fuel pump
2. Fuel injector unit
3. Fuel-flow divider
4. Individual fuel injection nozzles

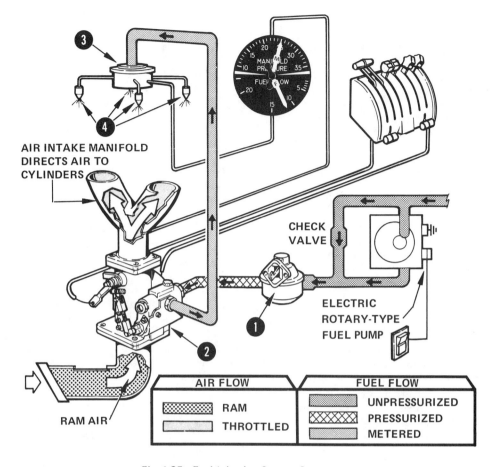

Fig. 1-25. Fuel Injection System Components

Fuel is delivered from the airplane's tanks to the engine-driven fuel pump, where the fuel is put under pressure. The pressurized fuel is routed through the fuel injector unit, where the fuel flow is metered by a set of valves according to the mixture setting and flow of air to the engine. Also, the intake airflow is throttled in the fuel injector unit. The metered fuel then is sent to the fuel-flow divider, where it is divided equally among the individual fuel lines that lead to each cylinder. The fuel lines carry the metered and divided fuel to the individual discharge nozzles where the fuel is atomized, then vaporized at the cylinder's intake port.

ENGINE-DRIVEN FUEL PUMP

The engine-driven fuel pump is the only constantly moving part in the continuous flow fuel injection system. This fuel pump is attached to the engine's accessory drive section. An electric fuel pump also is incorporated to provide fuel pressure for engine starting and to deal with possible failure of the engine-driven pump.

FUEL INJECTOR UNIT

The function of the fuel injector unit is similar to that of the carburetor in a conventional fuel-air induction system. The difference is that the fuel and air are

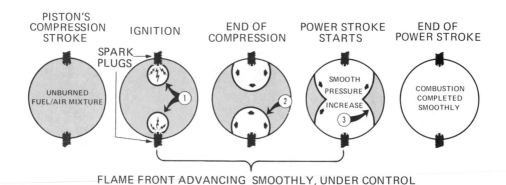

Fig. 1-26. Normal Combustion Process

not combined in the fuel injector unit. Instead, this unit regulates the air flowing through the air induction manifold and meters the correct amount of fuel required for the fuel injectors.

FUEL-FLOW DIVIDER

The fuel-flow divider, sometimes termed the fuel manifold, is designed to divide the fuel evenly between each of the cylinders. Valves are built into the flow divider to provide a positive fuel shutoff mechanism when the mixture control is moved to idle cutoff.

FUEL INJECTION NOZZLES

The fuel nozzles inject the metered fuel into the air induction manifold. Injection actually occurs in the cylinder head, just outside the intake valves and ports leading to the combustion chambers. The fuel is mixed with the intake air just before entering the combustion chamber.

FUEL-FLOW INDICATOR

A fuel-flow indicator enables the pilot to monitor the operation of the system, as well as determine the extent to which the mixture may be leaned. The fuel-flow indicator is actually a pressure gauge connected to the fuel manifold. The pressure gauge is marked in both pounds per square inch and gallons or pounds of fuel flow per hour.

DETONATION

Detonation is the uncontrolled, explosive combustion of fuel. The rate of burning is extremely rapid, producing excessive pressure and temperature within the engine. Detonation can cause the immediate failure of an engine by destroying a piston, valve, or part of the cylinder. Less severe detonation can cause overheating, loss of power, roughness, and reduced engine life.

The causes of detonation can be understood by first examining the normal combustion process, shown in figure 1-26. This figure depicts the inside of a cylinder, as seen through the top of the cylinder head during five phases of compression and combustion.

Normal combustion begins with the spark plugs igniting the fuel-air mixture as it is compressed in the cylinder (item 1). As the piston reaches the end of its compression stroke, two flame fronts are advancing evenly through the unburned fuel-air mixture toward the center of the cylinder (item 2). The fuel is burned in the area immediately behind the advancing flame front, as shown by the heavy lines (item 3). The evenly burning fuel causes a smooth increase in temperature and pressure. This increasing pressure provides the engine with a controlled amount of energy during the piston's power stroke.

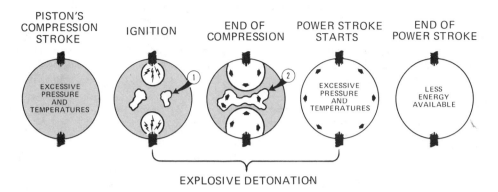

Fig. 1-27. Detonation

Detonation occurs when the fuel-air mixture is compressed at an abnormally high temperature and/or pressure, as illustrated in figure 1-27. As this mixture is ignited by the spark plugs and the flame front begins to advance across the cylinder, the temperature and pressure within the area of the unburned fuel-air mixture increases still further.

Eventually, the temperature and pressure become great enough to support explosive combustion and the fuel is ignited spontaneously (item 1). The resultant flame fronts advance erratically and rapidly (item 2), creating pressure increases which cause the engine to lose power. The pressure may build to such an extreme that it is in excess of the engine's structural capacity.

The following conditions are common causes of detonation and should be avoided.

1. Takeoff with an overheated engine
2. Operations with an extremely high manifold pressure and extremely low r.p.m.
3. Operations over 75 percent power with an extremely lean mixture

PREIGNITION

Preignition and detonation are interrelated, since preignition can cause detonation and detonation can cause preignition. Preignition is the premature burning of fuel, caused by a residual hotspot. As shown in figure 1-28, this hotspot can be a glowing piece of carbon deposit on a spark plug (item 1), or a cracked ceramic spark plug insulator.

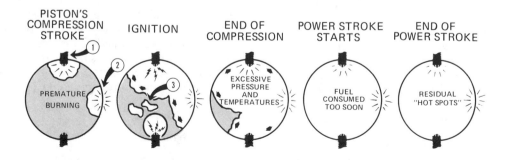

Fig. 1-28. Preignition

The rough edge of a valve, a broken piston ring, cracked piston, or scored cylinder wall may become incandescent and cause preignition (item 2). By the time normal ignition occurs, a large quantity of the fuel-air mixture has already been burned. The premature burning can easily lead to excessive pressures and temperatures. In turn, these factors can result in detonation (item 3).

EXHAUST GAS TEMPERATURE GAUGE

Some airplanes are equipped with an exhaust gas temperature gauge for each engine to aid in mixture adjustment. The EGT gauge measures the exhaust temperature at a point just outside the combustion chamber. The EGT sensor is a thermocouple-type probe made of dissimilar metals that generate a minute electrical current when heated. This probe is sensitive to temperature changes and provides an accurate means of determining the relative combustion temperatures. Thus, by using the EGT gauge, the mixture control (fuel-air ratio) for each engine can be adjusted with accuracy and efficiency.

After the power is reduced to the cruise power setting, the EGT may be used to lean the mixture. The mixture control is slowly moved toward the lean position while the movement of the EGT needle is noted. As the mixture is leaned, the EGT shows the increase in combustion temperatures. When the peak temperature is reached, the mixture is slowly enriched until a temperature decrease of approximately 100° Fahrenheit is noted. However, the pilot's operating handbook should be consulted for specific leaning techniques using the EGT gauge.

ALTERNATE AIR SOURCE

Fuel injection has the added advantage over float carburetion of being less susceptible to induction system icing. The refrigeration process in a carburetor is caused by both the cooling effect of the large pressure reduction in the throttle venturi and the heat loss during the fuel vaporization process. The fuel injection system allows the greatest cooling effect at the cylinder head, where icing is least likely to develop.

The induction air supply in a fuel injection system is filtered prior to entering the induction system air intake. The intake screen at the front of the cowling is a potential source of induction icing. To prevent engine failure due to an iced-over or unusually clogged intake filter, the induction air system of a fuel injected engine must have an alternate air source. The alternate air door may be opened by a manual control located inside the cabin. In addition to the manual control, some engine models have automatic doors which open if the normal air intake becomes obstructed.

ELECTRICAL SYSTEMS

Electrical power for most light and medium twin-engine airplanes is provided by a 14-volt or a 28-volt, direct current (DC), negative ground system. The generating system incorporates two engine-driven alternators and two voltage regulators. Each alternator circuit has an overvoltage relay which protects the electrical equipment in the event of a voltage regulator malfunction.

Included within the system is the battery, which may be either 12-volt or 24-volt, depending on the requirements of the system. Electrical power from the battery is used primarily for engine starting. However, it is also a source of emergency electrical power in the remote event both alternators should fail.

SYSTEM COMPONENTS

ALTERNATORS

The electrical power required by the system is supplied by two engine-driven alternators, one mounted on each engine. The initial electrical power that is produced is alternating current (AC), which is then converted to direct current (DC) for use by the electrical system. If the airplane is equipped with generators, this conversion process is unnecessary because generators initially produce DC electrical power.

Compared to the generator system, the alternator system has an operational advantage, since electrical power is available at lower engine speeds. A generator system requires a minimum engine r.p.m. of approximately 1,000 before the generator provides power to the system. Therefore, during situations when the engine speed is below generator operating speed, all electrical power is supplied by the battery. This condition creates a battery drain, and when the engine speed increases, the battery begins accepting a charge. The numerous cycles of battery charging and discharging over a period of time tend to shorten battery life.

VOLTAGE REGULATORS

The electrical power supplied by the alternators initially flows through the voltage regulators. A voltage regulator is provided for each alternator and serves two basic functions. First, when both engines are running, both alternators are producing electrical current. The voltage regulators maintain the proper electrical load-sharing between the two alternators. This eliminates one alternator from assuming too great an electrical load while the other has a lesser load. Second, the voltage regulators maintain a constant electrical system voltage. Depending upon the individual airplane and system requirements, the voltage is maintained to either 14.0 or 28.0 volts.

OVERVOLTAGE RELAYS

After the electrical power passes through the voltage regulator, it is routed to the overvoltage relay. This type of relay is provided within each alternator circuit to protect the electrical system from overvoltage malfunctions. If a malfunction occurs and the alternator output exceeds the normal 14.0 or 28.0 system voltage, the overvoltage relay trips and the alternator is taken off the line. Most light and medium twin-engine airplanes are equipped with warning lights to indicate that an overvoltage condition has occurred and an alternator is inoperative. If this condition occurs, the pilot's operating handbook should be consulted for the appropriate corrective action.

BUS BARS AND POWER DISTRIBUTION

Each electrical system incorporates bus bars to distribute the electrical power to each component of the electrical system. Depending upon the airplane's complexity, the number of bars within the electrical system may vary. The following discussion of bus bars and power distribution refers to figure 1-29, which traces electrical power from each alternator to the electrical components of the system.

Electrical power from each alternator passes through the voltage regulators and overvoltage relays enroute to the respective isolation bus bars (item 1). The power is then directed to the left and right electrical power bus bar (item 2). This bus bar divides the electrical power into two different circuits (items 3 and 4). By tracing these two circuits, it is seen that item 3 powers the number 1 bus bar and item 4 powers the number 2 bus bar. Once the electrical power reaches these bars, it is distributed to the individual electrical components on each bus. From the illustration it is seen that the bus bars simply distribute electrical power throughout the system.

In the event one alternator is inoperative, the other alternator will power all the required bus bars, as shown through the circuits of items 3 and 4 in the illustration. The electrical power bus bar in this situation distributes electrical power to both the number 1 and number 2 bus bars and no electrical components

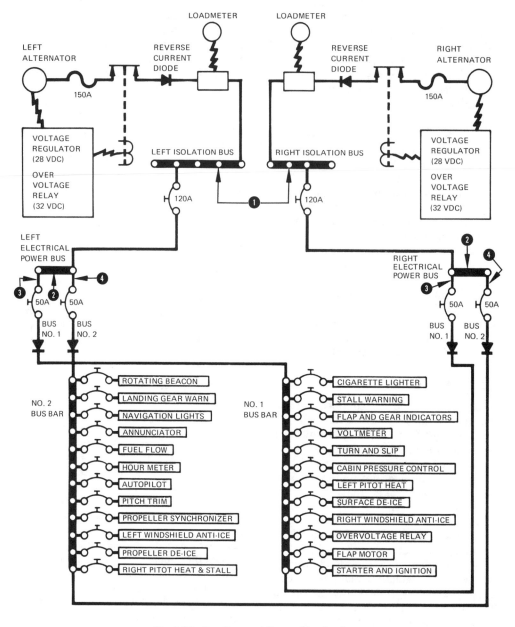

Fig. 1-29. Bus Bars and Power Distribution

are rendered inoperative due to alternator failure. Although not shown in the illustration, the airplane battery is connected to the left isolation bus bar. In the remote event both alternators fail, the battery will power all of the bus bars for a limited period of time.

CIRCUIT BREAKERS

Circuit breakers are installed to protect each component within the electrical system. In the event a sudden power surge or other malfunction occurs on a circuit, heat is generated and the circuit breaker is tripped automatically. The circuit breaker may be reset after a cooling period by simply pushing it back in place. However, if the breaker trips a second time, it should not be reset or held in place. The corresponding electrical circuit should be considered inoperative and the pilot's operating handbook consulted.

OPERATION WITH ONE ALTERNATOR INOPERATIVE

In the event one alternator fails or engine-out operations are required, certain considerations must be observed for single alternator operation. During this condition, all unnecessary electrical equipment should be turned off to avoid demanding excess current from the operating alternator. An overloaded alternator may fail and/or trip a circuit breaker.

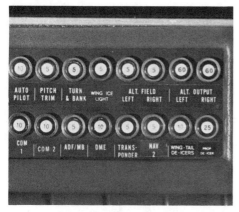

Fig. 1-30. Circuit Breakers

The following method can be used when it is necessary to reduce the electrical load. If the airplane is equipped with 60-ampere alternators, the maximum system load with both alternators operating is 120 amperes. With one alternator inoperative, the maximum system load is 60 amperes. To determine the amperage of each circuit, the pilot can refer to the numbers on circuit breakers as shown in figure 1-30. He should operate only the required equipment that does not have a total of more than 60 amperes. This

procedure precludes the possibility of demanding more amperage than the alternator is capable of producing.

LANDING GEAR SYSTEMS

The two types of landing gear systems commonly installed on multi-engine airplanes are hydraulic and electric. The difference between the two systems is simply that one uses hydraulic pressure and the other utilizes mechanical linkages from an electric motor to retract or extend the landing gear. Both types of systems incorporate safety features which include an emergency extension provision and a warning horn and lights to alert the pilot of unsafe conditions. Safety switches to prevent inadvertent gear retraction on the ground also are provided on most recently manufactured models.

HYDRAULIC GEAR SYSTEMS

Hydraulic landing gear systems incorporate either an electrically powered reversible pump or an engine-driven hydraulic pump. Each system uses a hydraulic reservoir and a series of pressure switches to regulate the pressure within the system. When the landing gear selector switch is placed in either the UP or DOWN position, the electrically powered or engine-driven hydraulic pump is put into operation. As shown by the example in figure 1-31, the pump directs hydraulic pressure to each actuating cylinder. As fluid pressure is exerted on one side of the cylinder, fluid on the other side is directed back to the hydraulic pump.

REGULATION OF SYSTEM PRESSURE

The hydraulic pump, whether it is engine-driven or electrically powered, is designed to operate within a specified pressure range. When excessive pressure is sensed, a relief valve incorporated within the pump opens and hydraulic fluid is routed back to the reservoir.

A second type of relief valve is installed to prevent excessive pressures due to

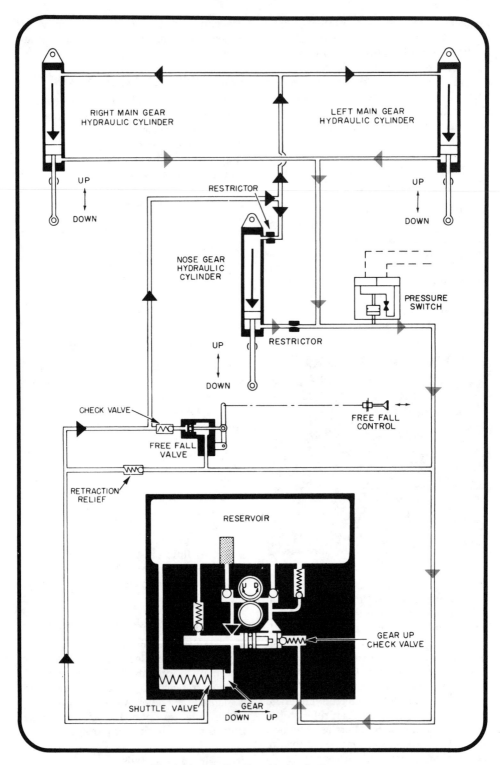

Fig. 1-31. Landing Gear Hydraulic System

thermal expansion. The location of this valve within the system varies between each make and model of airplane.

The hydraulic pressure is also regulated by the limit switches on each of the three landing gear. Each gear has one switch for extension and one switch for retraction. The purpose of these switches is to deenergize the hydraulic pump after the landing gear is either fully extended or retracted. In the event any of the limit switches should fail, a backup valve is installed to relieve excess pressure within the system.

ELECTRICAL GEAR SYSTEMS

Landing gear systems which are operated electrically utilize a reversible electric motor attached directly to a single gearbox. Each landing gear is connected mechanically to the gearbox through a series of linkages, as shown in figure 1-32. The electric motor is energized when the landing gear selector switch is placed in either the UP or DOWN posi-

tion and the landing gear is driven towards the selected position. The electric motor will continue to operate until the UP or DOWN limit switch on the gearbox disconnects the electrical power. This occurs when the gear is fully retracted or extended.

LANDING GEAR SAFETY FEATURES

POSITION LIGHTS

Position lights are common safety features for landing gear systems. The type incorporated in most multi-engine airplanes utilizes four lights—three green and one red. The three green lights indicate that all three landing gear are in the *down and locked* position. The red light illuminates when the gear is in transit or unsafe for landing. Consequently, when the landing gear is cycled up or down, it is normal for the red light to illuminate and then go off when the gear has been fully extended or retracted.

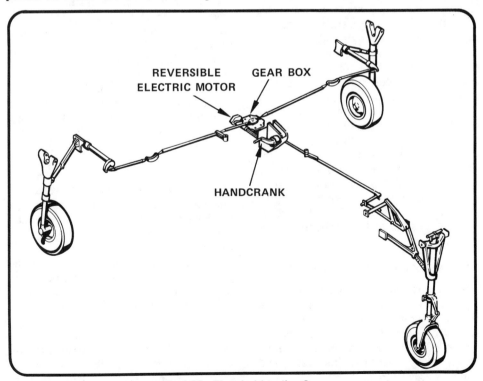

REVERSIBLE
ELECTRIC MOTOR

GEAR BOX

HANDCRANK

Fig. 1-32. Electrical Landing Gear

WARNING HORN

A landing gear warning horn is installed to advise the pilot of a potentially hazardous landing gear condition prior to landing. The warning horn also will sound if the landing gear selector switch is in the UP position while the airplane is on the ground. However, the main purpose of the horn is to alert the pilot in the event the gear is retracted or unsafe during the approach to landing.

When power is reduced, a throttle switch located in the power console actuates the warning horn if the landing gear is not down and locked. Generally, this switch is activated at 12 to 14 inches of manifold pressure. The warning horn will continue to operate until the landing gear is down and locked or the power is advanced.

SAFETY SWITCH

Most currently manufactured multi-engine airplanes are equipped with a landing gear safety switch which prevents the landing gear from retracting while the airplane is on the ground. This switch usually is located on the left main landing gear. A representative type is shown in figure 1-33. In the event the landing gear selector switch is inadvertently placed in the UP position while the airplane is on the ground, the safety switch prevents actuation of the landing gear power source. In this situation, the landing gear will not retract, but the landing gear warning horn will sound, warning the pilot of the improper position of the gear selector switch. Once the selector switch is placed in the proper DOWN position, the warning horn should silence.

EMERGENCY LANDING GEAR EXTENSION

In the event the power source for landing gear extension fails, an emergency gear *extension* feature is provided for each type of system. The methods of extension include the manual hand pump, CO$_2$ pressure, manual hand crank, or gravity freefall.

Fig. 1-33. Landing Gear Safety Switch

Landing gear systems which utilize an engine-driven hydraulic pump to extend the landing gear generally incorporate a manual hand pump. Through use of the hand pump, the pilot can produce system pressure to extend the gear. However, in the event of a leak in the hydraulic system, pressure cannot be maintained with the hand pump. For this reason, an independent CO$_2$ system may be provided on some models as a secondary emergency extension feature. When the system control is pulled, high pressure CO$_2$ flows from a storage cylinder through separate lines to the gear cylinders and forces the landing gear to the extended position. This type of emergency extension should only be used when all other means of lowering the landing gear have failed and when the gear can be left down for landing.

Landing gear systems which normally utilize an electric motor and mechanical linkages to extend the gear incorporate a mechanical hand crank for emergency extension. When extended and engaged for operation, the hand crank is connected to the gearbox and the landing gear may be extended manually by turning the crank. This process normally requires 50 to 55 revolutions of the hand crank.

The last method of emergency extension to be discussed in this section is the gravity freefall system. This type of

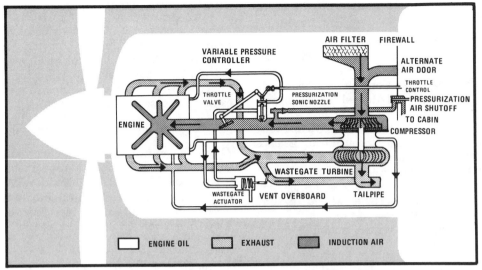

Fig. 1-34. Turbocharger System Components

extension system is incorporated in air-planes which utilize hydraulic pressure to hold the landing gear in the retracted position. For this type of gear, the only requirement for extension is to relieve the pressure within the system. An emergency gear extension knob in the cabin controls the freefall valve. The knob can be pulled to release hydraulic pressure so the gear can free fall to the DOWN position. Gravity, in conjunction with aerodynamic loads, extends and locks the gear. The pilot should be aware that if the hydraulic system develops a leak or if hydraulic pressure is relieved for any reason, gravity will cause the landing gear to extend.

TURBOCHARGING

Control of atmospheric pressure in the induction system goes hand in hand with control of fuel induction and vaporization. Unfortunately, atmospheric pressure varies from location to location and decreases with an increase in altitude. Any decrease in the intake manifold pressure causes a decrease in engine power output. Pressurization of the air in the intake manifold as the airplane climbs to altitude is one solution to this power loss.

SYSTEM COMPONENTS

The turbocharger consists of two separate components—a compressor and a turbine—connected by a common shaft, as illustrated in figure 1-34. The turbine-driven compressor supplies pressurized air to the engines for high altitude operation. The compressor and its housing are located between the ambient air intake and the induction air manifold. The turbine assembly is part of the exhaust system and utilizes the flow of exhaust gases to drive the compressor.

WASTEGATE

The automatic wastegate actuator is operated by engine oil pressure and activates a wastegate valve in the exhaust bypass. Oil pressure closes the wastegate and all the exhaust gas is routed into the turbine side of the turbocharger, giving maximum compression to induction air. When the actuator opens the wastegate, a minimum of exhaust gas drives the turbocharger. The balance of the exhaust is dumped overboard. Thus, the wastegate position regulates the compressed air available to the engine.

The following steps illustrate the operation of the system.

1. Induction air is taken in through the air filter and ducted to the compressor.
2. The induction air is then compressed and ducted to the engine.
3. As the wastegate opens, some of the exhaust gases are routed around the turbine, through the exhaust bypass, then overboard.
4. When the wastegate is closed, all of the exhaust gases pass through and drive the turbine, which, in turn, drives the compressor.
5. The exhaust gases are dumped overboard.

VARIABLE ABSOLUTE PRESSURE CONTROLLER

The control center of the turbocharger system is the variable absolute pressure controller. This device simplifies turbocharging to one control—the throttle. Once the pilot has set the desired manifold pressure, virtually no throttle adjustment is required with changes in altitude. The controller senses manifold pressure requirements for various altitudes and regulates the oil pressure to adjust the wastegate. Thus, the turbocharger maintains only the manifold pressure called for by the throttle setting, except for operation above the critical altitude, where the wastegate reaches the fully closed position. The *critical altitude* is that altitude above which the maximum rated manifold pressure cannot be obtained at full throttle.

OPERATIONAL CHARACTERISTICS

Aside from the absence of manifold pressure variation with altitude, there is little difference between the turbocharged and the nonturbocharged engine when operated below the critical altitude. Above critical altitude, certain operational characteristics must be understood to fully realize the advantages and capabilities of this turbocharger/engine combination.

R.P.M. AND MANIFOLD PRESSURE

Above the critical altitude, any change in r.p.m. will result in a change in manifold pressure. A decrease in r.p.m. will produce an increase in manifold pressure. Conversely, an increase in r.p.m. will cause a decrease in manifold pressure.

FUEL FLOW AND MANIFOLD PRESSURE

Above the critical altitude, with r.p.m. and manifold pressure established for cruise, leaning will cause a slight increase in manifold pressure. When the mixture reaches the recommended fuel flow, a slight reduction in manifold pressure may be necessary.

AIRSPEED AND MANIFOLD PRESSURE

Above the critical altitude, an increase in airspeed will result in a corresponding increase in manifold pressure. This is true because the increase in ram air pressure from an increase in airspeed is magnified by the compressor, resulting in an increase in manifold pressure. The increase in manifold pressure creates a higher airflow through the engine, causing higher turbine speeds and increasing manifold pressure. This characteristic may be used to best advantage by allowing the aircraft to accelerate to cruise speed after leveling off and prior to reducing power.

ENGINE RESPONSE AT HIGH ALTITUDE

Sudden, large power changes at altitude with rich mixtures can cause loss of engine power. Power changes should be made slowly, with necessary mixture adjustments in a series of two or three steps.

OVERBOOST CONTROL

The engine incorporates a relief valve in the induction system which is set to relieve any excess manifold pressure that may develop. This valve will open only in the event of a malfunction in the variable absolute pressure control system.

To avoid exceeding normal manifold pressure limits, particularly in cold weather, the last 1-1/2 inches of throttle should be applied slowly while observing manifold pressures. A momentary over-boost to the limit of the relief valve will have no detrimental effect on the engine, but is indicative of a malfunctioning variable absolute pressure controller. If overboost is more than momentary or occurs when engine oil temperature is normal, the controller should be checked at an authorized facility.

ICE CONTROL EQUIPMENT AND SYSTEMS

The increased need for utilization of aircraft during all weather conditions has led to the development of de-icing and anti-icing equipment. *De-icing* means removal, while *anti-icing* refers to ice prevention. Structural ice control equipment normally is installed to protect the propeller, wing and tail surfaces, windshield, pitot tube, and fuel vents. Some aircraft also make use of shielded antennas to insure adequate reception and transmission, and wing lights to illuminate areas of possible ice accumulation on the wings. The following discussion of ice control equipment, installations, and general operations pertains to systems which are typical of most light and medium twin-engine aircraft used in general aviation.

ELECTRICAL PROPELLER DE-ICING

The electrical propeller de-icing system employs heating elements to reduce the adhesion between the ice and the propeller. With the system in operation in icing conditions, the heating elements soften the layer of ice adhering to the propeller blades. Centrifugal force and airflow over the propeller cause the ice to be thrown from the blades.

HEATING ELEMENTS

The heating elements consist of heater wires enclosed in rubber pads. To provide additional strength, the rubber pads incorporate fabric plies similar to those used in tires. The dull, porous side of the rubber pad is cemented to the leading edge of the propeller blade. The area covered extends from the blade root part way along the leading edge. The outer portion of the heating pad has a very smooth, glossy surface which reduces ice adherence. A propeller with heating pads is shown in figure 1-35.

Fig. 1-35. Propeller Heat Elements

The heating pad contains two elements—an inboard heater (near the propeller hub) and an outboard heater. These heating elements are activated individually and cycled on and off periodically by a timer. The cycling process of each heating element allows a slight ice accumulation which normally is removed when the heating cycle is repeated.

TIMER

In most installations, a timer is used to cycle the electrical current between the right and left propeller heating elements every minute, creating a two-minute cycle. In a given one-minute period, the outboard heaters of the right propeller operate for 30 seconds, followed by a 30-second operation of the inboard heaters. During the next minute, the left propeller heating elements operate in the same manner.

SLIP RINGS AND BRUSHES

A slip ring and brush assembly is utilized to provide electrical energy to the heat-

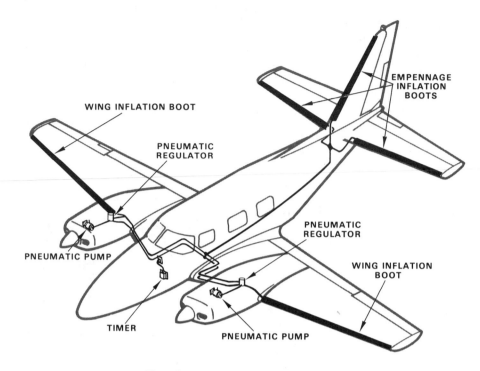

Fig. 1-36. Pneumatic De-Icing System

ing elements of the rotating propeller. Electricity is transferred by brushes which make contact with the slip ring as the propeller rotates.

AMMETER

The ammeter in this system provides a means of checking heater operation. In a three-bladed propeller system, the ammeter should indicate approximately 14 to 18 amperes when the system is in use. In addition, the timer cycles every 30 seconds, causing a current fluctuation which is reflected by the ammeter. This fluctuation indicates correct operation.

WING DE-ICING AND ANTI-ICING EQUIPMENT

Wing de-icing and anti-icing equipment normally falls within two categories—pneumatic boots and heated wings. Pneumatic boots break ice from the wing by expanding and the heated wing pre-

vents ice formation by channeling hot air through the wing's leading edge. The pneumatic system is found primarily on light and medium weight aircraft, while the heated wing system normally is used on jet aircraft.

PNEUMATIC DE-ICING SYSTEM

A typical pneumatic wing de-icing system is shown in figure 1-36. This system consists of the following components.

1. Inflation boots
2. Timer
3. Pneumatic regulators
4. Engine-driven pressure and vacuum sources

Inflation Boots

The inflation boots are fabric-reinforced rubber sheets containing inflation tubes. The boots are cemented to the leading edges of the wings, horizontal stabilizer, and vertical stabilizer. When the de-icing switch is turned on, all of the boots operate simultaneously.

In normal operation, the boots are held in the deflated position by slight vacuum pressure. As the system is energized, approximately 18 p.s.i. of positive pressure is applied to the inflation tubes. This pressure inflates the boots, as shown in figure 1-37, separating the ice from the leading edge. The airflow over the airfoil carries the ice away.

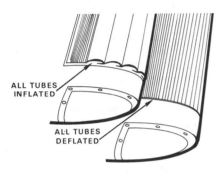

ALL TUBES INFLATED

ALL TUBES DEFLATED

Fig. 1-37. Pneumatic De-Icing Boots

The de-icing boots should not be operated until one-half to one inch of ice has accumulated on the airfoil's leading edge. If the boots are operated with less ice accumulation, they will tend to mold the ice to the new shape, rather than breaking it from the surface. If this occurs, ice will accumulate on the contour formed by the inflated boot and further operation of the de-icing system will have no effect.

Timer

When the de-icing switch is activated, the timer energizes the pneumatic pressure control valves for five to eight seconds. During this interval, pressure is applied to the inflation tubes, resulting in expansion of boots. Then, the timer automatically deenergizes the control valves, permitting the pressurized air to be exhausted overboard. The cycle is completed when a vacuum is reapplied to the boots, holding them in the deflated position.

Pneumatic Regulators

Pneumatic regulators are the heart of the wing de-icing system. Through a network of solenoids and control valves, the regulators govern the pressure and distribution of air in the system. The pneumatic regulators also control the pressure for the airplane instruments and other aircraft equipment.

Pressure and Vacuum Source

The wing de-icing system utilizes a pneumatic pump located on each engine. In case of a single pump failure, the remaining pump will supply adequate pressure and vacuum to operate the gyro flight instruments and wing de-icing systems.

HEATED WING ANTI-ICING SYSTEM

The heated wing anti-icing system often is found on turbojet or turboprop aircraft because the jet engine has a ready source of hot air to heat the wing. In this system, hot air is bled from one of the later stages of the compressor section of the engine and channeled to the aircraft wings.

The leading edge is enclosed and becomes a heated chamber. As the hot air from the engines flows through this chamber, it warms the leading edge to a temperature above freezing, preventing ice formation. A typical heated wing is illustrated in figure 1-38.

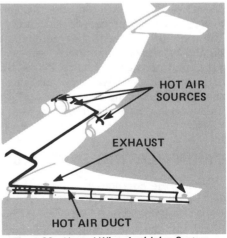

HOT AIR SOURCES

EXHAUST

HOT AIR DUCT

Fig. 1-38. Heated Wing Anti-Icing System

ELECTRICALLY HEATED WINDSHIELD

Most aircraft are equipped with a defroster consisting of vents which direct hot air across the windshield on the inside of the cabin. Although this system is adequate for some operations, flight in icing conditions may cause ice to adhere to the windshield, severly restricting visibility. The electrically heated windshield has been developed to combat this problem.

In this system, heat wires are embedded either in the windshield or in a piece of transparent material which is bonded to the windshield. In either system, electrical current flowing through the wires heats the windshield and prevents ice formation. To prevent overheating of the windshield, the system should be operated only during flight. If the windshield overheats, it may become "milky" in appearance and greatly reduce visibility.

OPERATION OF ICE CONTROL EQUIPMENT

Both anti-icing and de-icing equipment should be checked prior to flight whenever icing conditions are anticipated. In addition to ground checks, the pilot should cycle the wing de-icing boots and visually check for correct operation. During this time, the electric propeller de-icer can be turned on and the ammeter observed for proper indications. The prevention (anti-icing) equipment should be turned on prior to entering icing conditions or at the first indication of icing. This is necessary because most anti-icing equipment must "heat up" to normal operating temperatures before it is effective.

CABIN HEATING SYSTEMS

Although the components of each heating, ventilating, and defrosting system are basically identical, differences are found in the two methods of heat origination and regulation. The first type of system incorporates a gasoline combustion type heater and the second uses a simple heat exchanger mounted on each engine exhaust manifold.

GASOLINE COMBUSTION HEATER

The gasoline combustion heater is used on some makes and models of twin-engine airplanes as the source of cabin heat. The heater is usually located in the nose of the airplane and receives its fuel supply from the airplane fuel system.

Fresh air enters through the nose of the airplane and is routed through the heater. When the airplane is on the ground, a fan forces the heated air to the heat outlets or the defroster ducts in the cabin. After takeoff, the fan is deactivated automatically when the landing gear is retracted, and ram air provides heat circulation.

A thermostat usually is located in the duct just aft of the heater. When the temperature of the heated air exceeds the setting of the thermostat, it opens automatically and shuts off the heater. When the heated air cools to the thermostat setting, the heater starts again. Thus, the heater cycles on and off to maintain an even air temperature.

MANIFOLD HEAT EXCHANGER

In other models, cabin and defrost heat is provided by a heat exchanger mounted on the exhaust manifold of each engine. Outside air enters the system through a scoop on the engine cowling, passes through the heat exchanger, and is heated by the exhaust manifold. A combination heater and defroster valve, located in the forward side of the firewall, directs heated air for the cabin interior through a fresh air and temperature control valve assembly. At this point in the system, the temperature is regulated before the heat enters the cabin interior. This regulation is not accomplished by an automatic thermostat, but rather, by adding cool, outside air to the heated air.

A manual control inside the airplane regulates the amount of outside air mixed with the heated air.

The heated air that is routed through the heat and defroster valve for defrosting purposes does not go through the temperature control valve assembly. It is passed directly from the heat and defroster valve to the defroster outlet located at the base of the windshield. The defroster has a separate control lever that can be turned off when its operation is not required. When both the cabin heat and the defroster controls are off, heated air from the heat exchanger is dumped overboard.

chapter 2

PERFORMANCE CONSIDERATIONS

INTRODUCTION

Weight, balance, and performance information for multi-engine airplanes is more extensive and generally more complex than for single-engine airplanes. For this reason, it is essential that applicants for the multi-engine rating be thoroughly familiar with performance considerations. This chapter points out the distinctive aspects of multi-engine weight and balance control and illustrates the charts and tables which are necessary for determining various performance values.

NOTE:
Manufacturers have long recognized the need to standardize pilots' operating handbooks. Guidelines to achieve this standardization have been formulated, and recently manufactured multi-engine airplanes utilize the improved operating handbooks. One of the significant changes is that performance speeds are presented in knots. Weight and balance and performance chart formats have also changed in some cases. This chapter illustrates a cross section of typical multi-engine charts and includes samples of both old and new formats.

SECTION A—WEIGHT AND BALANCE

Flight operations must be conducted within the weight and balance limitations imposed by the manufacturer. When either weight or balance exceed limits, performance cannot be accurately predicted. Since neither the manufacturer nor the FAA can provide reliable performance data when certification limits are exceeded, the weight and balance condition of an airplane should be checked carefully prior to departure.

WEIGHT

There are several *standard aircraft weights* designated for weight and balance computations. However, there is some diversity in terminology based on the various manufacturers' preferences or the particular period of manufacture. For the purposes of this discussion, the following aircraft weights are considered.

1. Maximum gross weight
2. Maximum takeoff weight
3. Maximum landing weight
4. Maximum zero fuel weight
5. Basic empty weight

The *maximum gross weight* is computed by the manufacturer through extensive studies in stress analysis, and static and flight testing. These tests insure that the airplane can be operated safely when loaded and flown within the maximum gross weight limits.

Most manufacturers also designate maximum takeoff and landing weights. The *maximum takeoff weight* is the highest weight approved for the start of the takeoff run. The *maximum landing weight* is the highest weight approved for the landing touchdown and is generally based on the strength of the landing gear or other related structural components.

The manufacturer may specify a *maximum zero fuel weight* on some airplanes to limit the ratio of loads between the fuselage and wings. The maximum load that an airplane can carry also depends on the way the load is distributed in the airplane. The weight of an airplane in flight is supported largely by the wings; therefore, as the load carried in the fuselage is increased, the bending moment on the wings is increased. An airplane might safely carry 2,000 pounds if 1,400 pounds were carried in the fuselage and 600 pounds of fuel were in the wings. However, 2,000 pounds might be an unsafe load if the weight distribution were 1,600 pounds in the fuselage and 400 pounds in the wings. The excessive bending moment imposed on the wings by the 1,600 pounds in the fuselage might exceed the strength of related structural components. By observing the maximum zero fuel weight, a safe ratio of loads between the fuselage and wings can be maintained.

The *basic empty weight* includes the weight of a standard airplane, all optional equipment, unusable fuel, and full operating fluids, including full oil. This is the most convenient weight for beginning weight and balance computations.

NOTE:
Airplanes manufactured in past years may specify a licensed empty weight rather than a basic empty weight. Licensed empty weight does not include full oil. When operating such an airplane, it is beneficial to add the oil weight to the licensed empty weight to arrive at the basic empty weight. This will simplify weight and balance computations.

GROSS WEIGHT COMPUTATIONS

The following items should be used to compute gross weight.

1. Basic empty weight
2. Payload
   a. Occupants/cargo
   b. Baggage
3. Usable fuel

The basic empty weight is found in the weight and balance records. The sample record in figure 2-1 reflects the continuous history of changes in airplane structure and/or equipment that affect the weight and balance of the airplane. The latest entry for basic empty weight should be used. After this weight is located, it is entered in reference 1 of the weight and balance form, as shown in figure 2-2.

The *payload* normally consists of the occupants/cargo and baggage. It is always best to use the actual weight of the pilot and passengers for a flight, especially when close to the weight and balance limits. However, in the absence of actual weights, the following guidelines may be used: 170 pounds for an adult with an average physical stature and 80 pounds for children between the ages of 2 and 12. The actual weights for

PERFORMANCE CONSIDERATIONS

WEIGHT AND BALANCE RECORD
(CONTINUOUS HISTORY OF CHANGES IN STRUCTURE OR EQUIPMENT
AFFECTING WEIGHT AND BALANCE)

DATE	ITEM IN	OUT	DESCRIPTION OF ARTICLE OR MODIFICATION	ADDED (+) WT (LB)	ARM (IN)	MOMENT /100	REMOVED (−) WT (LB)	ARM (IN)	MOMENT /100	BASIC EMPTY WEIGHT WT (LB)	MOMENT /100
5/27			BASIC EMPTY WT							3464.2	1223.3
8/3		X	ALTIMETER, FT & MILLIBARS LH				1.1	13.5	.15	3463.1	1223.2
8/3	X		400 ENCODING ALTIMETER — IN	2.6	13.0	.34				3465.7	1223.5
8/3	X		400 GLIDE SLOPE INSL	2.9	-50.0	-1.45				3468.6	1222.1
8/3	X		RECEIVER R-443B	2.4	-63.0	-1.51				3471.0	1220.6
8/3	X		MOUNT 36450	0.9	-63.0	-.57				3471.9	1220.0
8/3	X		ANTENNA RGS-10-48	0.1	-92.0	-.09				3472.0	1220.1

OLD BASIC EMPTY WEIGHT 3,464.2 — OLD TOTAL MOMENT 122,330 — OLD CG 35.31 IN.
NEW BASIC EMPTY WEIGHT 3,472.0 — NEW TOTAL MOMENT 122,010 — NEW CG 35.14 IN.

Fig. 2-1. Weight and Balance Record

baggage and cargo must be used, since it is impossible to formulate a standard weight. These computations are made on the left side of the weight and balance form, as illustrated in figure 2-2. After the payload is totaled, it is transferred to reference 2 and added to the basic empty weight. This provides the zero fuel weight, or total weight before fuel loading, as depicted in reference 3. This

SAMPLE WEIGHT AND BALANCE FORM

PAYLOAD COMPUTATIONS				REF	ITEM		WEIGHT	MOMENT/100
ITEM OCCUPANTS OR CARGO	ARM	WEIGHT	MOMENT/100	1.	BASIC EMPTY WEIGHT		3,472	
				2.	PAYLOAD		800	
Seat 1		190		3.*	ZERO FUEL WEIGHT (sub-total) (Do not exceed maximum zero fuel weight)		4,272	
Seat 2		150						
Seat 3		170						
Seat 4		150		4.	FUEL LOADING	(main)	600	
Seat 5		—				(auxiliary)	378	
Seat 6		—				(wing lockers)	- --	
BAGGAGE		140		5.*	TAKEOFF WEIGHT		5,250	
PAYLOAD		800						
				6.	LESS FUEL TO DESTINATION	(main)	155	
						(auxiliary)	378	
						(wing lockers)	- - -	
				7.*	LANDING WEIGHT		4,717	

Fig. 2-2. Weight and Balance Form

value should not exceed the maximum zero fuel weight specified in the pilot's operating handbook. Any weight in excess of this amount must be comprised of fuel.

The total weight of the usable fuel is determined by multiplying the number of gallons by six pounds. Once computed, the fuel weight is entered in reference 4. The final figure for takeoff weight is found by totaling the zero fuel weight and fuel loading items, as determined in reference 5. The landing weight is determined by subtracting the fuel required to fly to the destination. Once the weight and balance form is complete, the takeoff weight is checked against the maximum takeoff weight in the limitations section of the pilot's operating handbook to insure the airplane is loaded within limits.

ADJUSTING GROSS WEIGHT

If the maximum allowable weight limit is exceeded, it must be reduced prior to flight and before a check can be made on the center of gravity. There are three items of the useful load which can be varied to reduce weight—fuel, baggage, or passengers/cargo.

The selection of one or more of these possibilities depends on the requirements for the flight. If conditions are such that all passengers and their baggage need to go on the flight, the fuel requirements must be calculated carefully and reduced to the minimum required for safe operation.

It is important to realize that the maximum gross weight is a legal limit. Above this weight, test information is not available and structural damage may occur. An airplane loaded above the weight limitations requires a longer takeoff run to become airborne because of two factors. First, the excess weight causes slower acceleration; and second, the airplane must be accelerated to a greater speed to provide the additional lift re-

quired. The climb performance is reduced even more because of the added weight. In extreme cases, the airplane may be unable to climb out of ground effect. Although a takeoff may be possible due to the extra lift available when in ground effect, the lift needed to sustain a climb may not be available.

In a cruise configuration, the overweight airplane must maintain a higher angle of attack, requiring a higher power setting and causing greater fuel consumption. During the landing approach, a higher airspeed must be maintained, resulting in a longer landing roll. In addition, the loss of an engine in an overloaded airplane makes performance very difficult to predict.

BALANCE

There are several terms which are used when making balance computations. They are included in the following list.

1. Center of gravity
2. Reference datum
3. Arm
4. Moment

The *center of gravity* (CG) is the point at which an airplane would balance if suspended. Its distance from the reference datum is found by dividing the total moment, explained below, by the total weight of the airplane.

The *reference datum* is an imaginary vertical plane from which all horizontal distances are measured for balance purposes. The datum location is arbitrarily specified by the manufacturer. It may be at the firewall, the nose, or a point in space in front of the aircraft. In any case, it lies along the longitudinal axis. Regardless of the placement, all moments aft of the datum have positive values, while all moments forward of this reference have negative values.

An *arm* is the horizontal distance from the reference datum to the center of

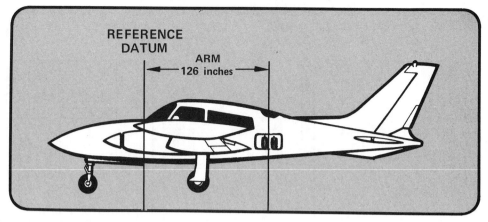

Fig. 2-3. Arm

gravity of an item, as illustrated in figure 2-3. For example, if a suitcase were placed in the baggage compartment 126 inches aft of the datum, it would have an arm of 126.

The *moment* is the product of the weight of an item multiplied by its arm. If the suitcase in the previous example weighed 25 pounds, it would have a moment of 3,150 pound-inches.

As long as these factors are used to insure the airplane is loaded within the CG limits designated by the manufacturer, all performance and flight characteristics will be normal. The airplane will be stable in flight and responsive to the controls. However, improper loading can cause detrimental flight effects.

FORWARD CG EFFECTS

An airplane that is loaded with the CG forward of limits requires a greater amount of elevator or stabilator pressure to break ground on takeoff. During climb and cruise flight, the additional back pressure required will decrease the cruise speed and climb capabilities. On a landing approach, an airplane loaded forward of limits may contact the ground with the nosewheel before the main gear, even though full aft elevator or stabilator control is used.

AFT CG EFFECTS

As the CG moves aft of limits, the airplane loses more and more stability. An airplane loaded aft of limits has a tendency to break ground on takeoff at very low airspeeds and initiate high attitude climbs. This condition may cause a stall. During climb and cruise flight, the airplane may be hard to control, since the nose may tend to oscillate up and down. Problems caused by the CG being out of limits can be eliminated through careful balance computations.

CENTER OF GRAVITY COMPUTATIONS

There are several methods in common use for determining an airplane's center of gravity. Since the basic computation method generally is considered too cumbersome for multi-engine airplanes, this discussion will be limited to the following list.

1. Tabular method
2. Graph method
3. Computer/plotter method

TABULAR METHOD

The *tabular method* utilizes weight and moment tables like those shown in figure 2-4. These tables are found in the pilot's operating handbook or the weight and balance papers. Once the information is

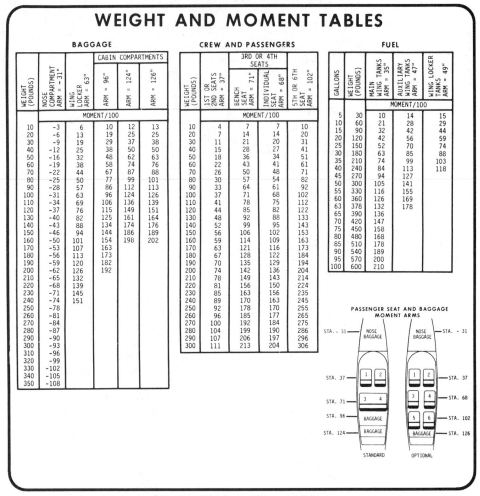

Fig. 2-4. Weight and Moment Tables

obtained from the table, it is transferred to a weight and balance form similar to the one depicted in figure 2-5.

First, the weights of each item are entered and the moment arms are determined from the passenger seat and baggage diagram. Next, the weight and moment tables are used to determine the total moment. On these tables, the moment values are divided by 100 to reduce the size of the numbers. Finally, the total moment is divided by the total weight to determine the CG location (212,800 lb.-in. ÷ 5,250 lbs. = 40.5 in.).

Now that the CG has been computed, it is necessary to determine if it is within prescribed limits, as indicated by the shaded area of figure 2-6. Since the CG computed was 40.5 inches at a gross weight of 5,250 pounds, it is within limits.

GRAPH METHOD

Another approach to computing the center of gravity is the *graph method*. The moments on the loading graph shown in figure 2-7 are divided by 1,000, making the information easy to read and use. The loading graph is an alternative

SAMPLE WEIGHT AND BALANCE FORM

PAYLOAD COMPUTATIONS				REF	ITEM		WEIGHT	MOMENT/100
ITEM OCCUPANTS OR CARGO	ARM	WEIGHT	MOMENT/100	1.	BASIC EMPTY WEIGHT		3472	1220
				2.	PAYLOAD		800	520
Seat 1	37	190	70	3.	* ZERO FUEL WEIGHT (sub-total) (Do not exceed maximum zero fuel weight)		4272	1740
Seat 2	37	150	56					
Seat 3	68	170	116					
Seat 4	68	150	102	4.	FUEL LOADING	(main)	600	210
Seat 5						(auxiliary)	378	178
Seat 6						(wing lockers)	---	---
BAGGAGE	126	140	176	5.	* TAKEOFF WEIGHT		5250	2128
PAYLOAD	---	800	520	6.	LESS FUEL TO DESTINATION	(main)	155	54
						(auxiliary)	378	178
						(wing lockers)	---	---
				7.	* LANDING WEIGHT		4717	1896

Fig. 2-5. Weight and Balance Form

to the tabular method for determining moments.

The graph is used by entering it at the appropriate weight on the left, proceeding horizontally to the appropriate reference line, and then vertically down to read the moment/1,000 pound-inches. In figure 2-7, for example, the graph is entered at 340 pounds (item 1), the weight of the pilot and front seat passenger. This point is extended horizontally until it intersects the pilot and front passenger line (item 2). The moment of

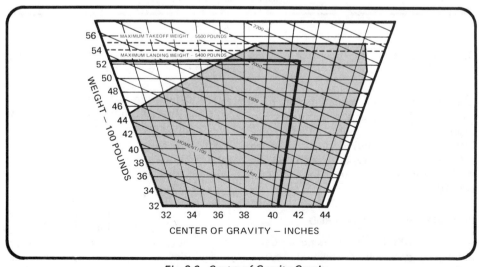

Fig. 2-6. Center of Gravity Graph

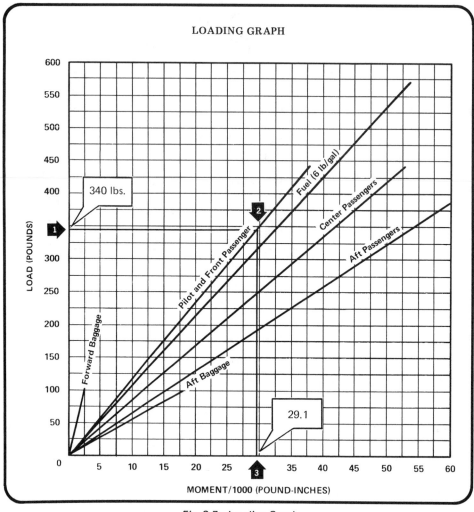

Fig. 2-7. Loading Graph

29.1 is read directly below this point (item 3).

This procedure is repeated for each individual item and the moments are recorded on the weight and balance form. The weights and moments then are totaled and the CG is determined by dividing the total moment by the total weight.

COMPUTER/PLOTTER METHOD

Another method requires a special computer/plotter which is designed for use with a specific type of airplane. This device has several advantages over other methods of weight and balance determination. For example, gross weight and CG location are determined simultaneously. In addition, calculations are much quicker and usually are more accurate because long, cumbersome multiplication and division problems are eliminated.

One side of the weight and balance plotter usually provides a list of general loading recommendations which initially allow the pilot to determine the most logical placement of loads. For example, when four people occupy the airplane,

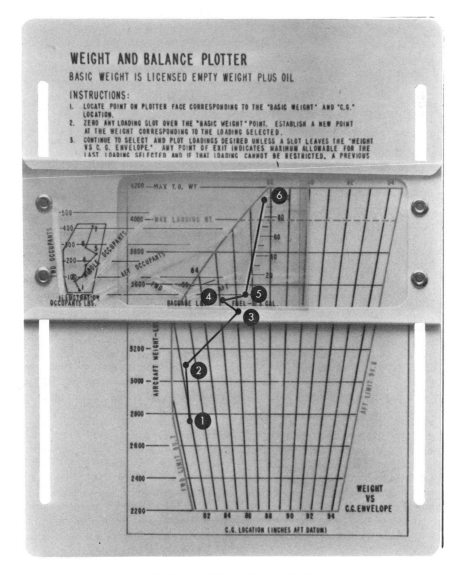

Fig. 2-8. Weight and Balance Plotter

the recommended loading may place two in the front seats and two in the middle seats. Similar recommendations for baggage and fuel loads also are specified.

The computation side of the weight and balance plotter is depicted in figure 2-8. This slide is precut with slots representing the total weight of the forward, middle, and aft occupants; the baggage in the forward and aft compartments; and the fuel in U.S. gallons. By marking through the slots onto the envelope, the effect on CG location for each compartment can be determined progressively.

Figure 2-8 also illustrates the solution to a typical problem under the following conditions.

Basic empty weight . . . . . 2,745 lbs.
Empty weight CG . . . . 82.0 in.

Pilot and front passenger . . 340 lbs.
Center seat passengers . . . . 340 lbs.
Forward baggage . . . . 50 lbs.
Aft baggage . . . . 50 lbs.
Fuel (95-gal. maximum) . . . 570 lbs.

The steps for solving this problem include the following items which correspond to the callouts in figure 2-8.

1. Locate the basic empty weight and center of gravity
2. Plot pilot and front passenger
3. Plot center seat passengers
4. Plot forward baggage
5. Plot aft baggage
6. Plot fuel

The gross weight and CG location fall within the envelope; therefore, the airplane meets weight and balance requirements. Additionally, as the fuel is used, the weight and CG will follow down the fuel line and stay within the envelope for landing.

CENTER OF GRAVITY SHIFT

After making weight and balance computations, the pilot may find that, although he is within allowable gross weight limits, he has exceeded his CG limits. In this case, he should be able to rapidly and accurately determine the minimum load shift needed to return the airplane to a safe flight condition. This is usually accomplished by shifting the passengers and/or baggage to more favorable locations.

For example, it is assumed that an airplane is loaded to 4,000 pounds, that the aft CG limit is 94.6 inches, and that the computed CG is 95.2 inches. From this, it can be determined that the CG is .6 inches aft of the limits (95.2 in. - 94.6 in. = .6 in.). Since the aft CG limits are exceeded, the *total aircraft moment must be reduced*. If the forward CG limits had been exceeded, it would have been necessary to *increase total aircraft moment*.

To determine the moment that must be reduced, the airplane's gross weight is multiplied by the distance the CG is aft of limits (4,000 lbs. x .6 in. = 2,400 lb.-in.). Next, it is determined where the weight can be shifted to reduce this moment. For example, if the airplane has both a forward and aft baggage compartment, some of the baggage in the aft compartment can be moved to the forward compartment. A typical distance between the two compartments might be 156.2 in.

The amount of weight to be shifted is determined by dividing the moment by the distance involved (2,400 lb.-in. ÷ 156.2 in. = 15.4 lbs.). To load the airplane within acceptable limits, approximately 15-1/2 pounds of baggage must be moved from the aft compartment to the forward compartment.

SECTION B—PERFORMANCE CHARTS

Through an approved pilot's operating handbook, manufacturers provide all of the performance information necessary to insure safe operation of an airplane. It is important for the prospective multi-engine pilot to become thoroughly familiar with the data this handbook contains. Concepts such as the accelerate-stop distance and single-engine climb performance are unique to multi-engine operations, and accurate computations of these and other values are important to safe operation.

PERFORMANCE FACTORS

There are several factors which affect aircraft performance, including density altitude, surface wind, runway condition, and gross weight. Normally, density altitude is the most significant factor because of its effect on engine performance, propeller efficiency, and lift generated by the wings.

DENSITY ALTITUDE

Density altitude is pressure altitude corrected for temperature deviations from the standard atmosphere. A pressure altitude of 29.92 inches of mercury at sea level and a temperature of 15° Celsius (59° Fahrenheit) are used to represent the standard atmosphere. These values are used by some manufacturers as a basis for plotting performance data. Under the newer performance chart formats, density altitude may not be used, since tables or graphs can be presented with pressure altitude and temperature in degrees Celsius. Essentially, these charts combine the density altitude problem with the performance problem.

DENSITY ALTITUDE DETERMINATION

When necessary, density altitude may be determined by using either a chart presentation or a computer. For example, when using a chart like the one shown in

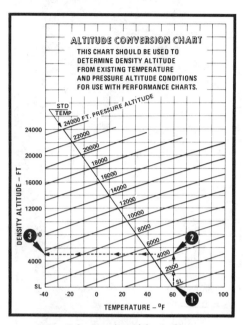

Fig. 2-9. Density Altitude Chart

figure 2-9, the first step is to enter the chart at the appropriate temperature. A temperature of 60° Fahrenheit and a pressure altitude of 4,000 feet are used for this example. The 60° Fahrenheit line (item 1) is followed upward to the diagonal line representing a 4,000-foot pressure altitude (item 2). The density altitude is then determined by moving to the left margin of the chart and reading 5,000 feet (item 3).

Another way to determine the density altitude is by using a computer. Referring to figure 2-10, the 60° Fahrenheit temperature is converted to 16° Celsius (item 1), since the computer requires use of degrees Celsius for density altitude computations. This temperature is placed opposite the pressure altitude of 4,000 feet (item 2). The resulting density altitude of 5,000 feet appears in the density altitude window (item 3).

HUMIDITY

Although humidity normally is not included in density altitude computations,

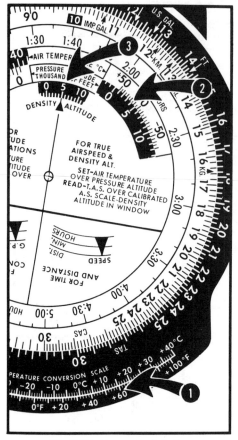

Fig. 2-10. Computer Solution

it should be noted that water vapor will increase takeoff distance and decrease climb performance. The rated horsepower of an engine is determined in dry air and standard atmospheric conditions. For this reason, as water vapor increases, air density decreases and the engine's power output decreases. This power loss can be as high as seven percent when the relative humidity is 100 percent.

SURFACE WIND

The surface wind direction and velocity also have a direct bearing on takeoff performance. Substantial headwinds shorten the takeoff run and compensate for some of the adverse effects of high density altitude. Conversely, a tailwind increases the takeoff run because a higher groundspeed is required for takeoff.

Since the wind seldom blows precisely down the runway, it often is necessary to determine the actual headwind component. This can be accomplished using a wind component chart.

RUNWAY CONDITIONS

Runway conditions are also a factor in takeoff performance, since most takeoff values are based on using a fully loaded airplane on a hard-surfaced, dry, level runway. Uphill gradients and soft or wet surfaces decrease takeoff performance. On the other hand, downhill gradients and hard or dry surfaces improve takeoff performance.

GROSS WEIGHT

Gross weight is the final factor that affects takeoff and climb performance. The takeoff performance information found on most single-engine airplane charts is based on maximum gross weight, since all conditions at a lesser weight will improve airplane performance. However, multi-engine performance information normally specifies additional weights which are less than the maximum gross weight to more accurately determine performance values when the airplane is operated at lighter weights.

PERFORMANCE CHARTS

Performance charts in the pilot's operating handbook provide a method of determining airplane performance for a given set of conditions. Although these charts vary in design between manufacturers, they generally are presented in either tabular or graphic displays. They also are presented to correspond to the normal chronological sequence of flight events.

TAKEOFF CHARTS

Takeoff charts follow the general information in the pilot's operating handbook and normally are quite detailed. A typical multi-engine takeoff chart is shown

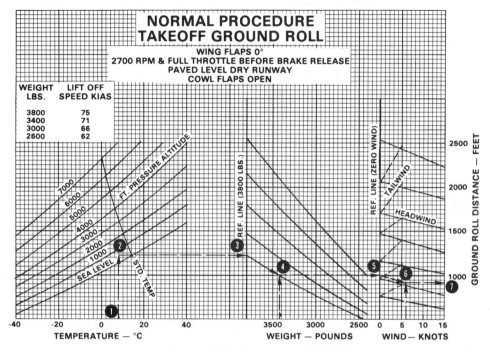

Fig. 2-11. 0° Flap Takeoff Ground Roll

in figure 2-11. From this chart, the pilot can determine the ground run required for a normal takeoff. A sample problem is based on the following conditions.

Flap configuration .... 0°
Temperature .... 8°C
Pressure altitude .... 680 ft.
Takeoff weight .... 3,430 lbs.
Headwind component .... 6 kts.
Liftoff speed................... 71 KIAS
Barrier speed .... 83 KIAS

The following procedure should be used to determine the ground run required for takeoff. The steps correspond to the numbered callouts on the chart.

1 Enter the chart at the outside air temperature line.

2 Move vertically to the appropriate pressure altitude line.

3 Move horizontally to the 3,800-pound maximum weight line.

4 Move diagonally to the actual airplane weight line of 3,430 pounds.

5 Move horizontally to the 0-knot line.

6 Move diagonally to the actual headwind component line of 6 knots.

7 Move horizontally to the ground roll distance of 820 feet.

ACCELERATE-STOP DISTANCE

Another important consideration when computing takeoff data is the accelerate-stop distance. This distance is the amount of runway required under existing conditions to accelerate to liftoff speed, experience an engine failure at that point, immediately discontinue the takeoff, and stop the airplane on the remaining runway. A typical accelerate-stop distance chart is depicted in figure 2-12. The dashed line indicates the solution to a sample problem, based on the information at the top of the chart and on the following conditions.

Gross weight .... 4,300 lbs.
Engine failure speed .... 81 KIAS
Pressure altitude .... 2,000 ft.
Temperature .... 20°C

ACCELERATE STOP DISTANCE

CONDITIONS:
1. Power - FULL THROTTLE and 2700 RPM Before Brake Release.
2. Mixtures - LEAN for field elevation.
3. Wing Flaps - UP.
4. Cowl Flaps - OPEN.
5. Level, Hard Surface, Dry Runway.
6. Engine Failure at Engine Failure Speed.
7. Idle Power and Heavy Braking After Engine Failure.

NOTE:
1. If full power is applied without brakes set, distances apply from point where full power is applied.
2. Decrease distance 3% for each 4 knots headwind.
3. Increase distance 5% for each 2 knots tailwind.

WEIGHT - POUNDS	ENGINE FAILURE SPEED - KIAS	PRESSURE ALTITUDE - FEET	TOTAL DISTANCE - FEET				
			-20°C -4°F	-10°C +14°F	0°C 32°F	+10°C +50°F	+20°C +68°F
4300	81	Sea Level	1730	1820	1920	202.	20..
		1000	1830	1940	2040	215.	2260
		2000	1950	2060	2170	2290	2410
			2070	2190	2310	2440	
			2210	2340	2470	2610	
		5000	2360	2500	2640	2790	2950
		6000	2520	2680	2830	2990	3160
		7000	2710	2870	3040	3220	3410
		8000	2910	3090	3280	3470	3680
		9000	3140	3340	3550	3760	4070
		10,000	3390	3610	3830	4150	4410

Fig. 2-12. Accelerate-Stop Distance Chart

The following procedure should be used to determine the accelerate-stop distance for a rejected takeoff. The steps correspond to the numbered callouts on the table.

1. Enter the chart at a gross weight of 4,300 pounds.
2. Proceed horizontally to the critical engine failure speed of 81 KIAS.
3. Move diagonally to the pressure altitude of 2,000 feet.
4. Move horizontally to the +20°C temperature column.
5. Read 2,410 feet, the accelerate-stop distance.

A 2,500-foot runway would be considered critical in this instance if the pilot desired optimum safety. It is important to note that the accelerate-stop distance shown by the chart assumes maximum braking on a paved, dry, level runway.

CLIMB RATE AND SPEED

After liftoff, the obstacle takeoff profile is to maintain the best angle of climb until clearing all obstacles, then lower the nose to let the airspeed increase to the best rate of climb. Most manufacturers recommend maintaining this airspeed until reaching a safe altitude, then making a transition to cruise climb.

The cruise climb is flown at a higher airspeed, which provides better over-the-nose visibility. The cruise climb also provides better engine cooling.

MULTI-ENGINE CLIMB

Figure 2-13 illustrates a typical two-engine climb chart and the corresponding rate of climb using maximum continuous power with the landing gear and flaps retracted. This chart is based on standard atmospheric conditions; therefore, performance values must be adjusted when conditions vary from standard (item 1). The chart also specifies the best climb speed for various gross weights. For example, at a gross weight of 5,000 pounds, the climb should be conducted at 128 m.p.h. indicated airspeed (item 2).

The dashed line on the chart shows the solution to a typical problem based on the following conditions.

Standard altitude . . . . . 14,000 ft.
Gross weight . . . . 5,000 lbs.
Temperature . . . . 19°F

The two-engine rate of climb is found by entering the chart at the standard altitude of 14,000 feet (item 3), then moving horizontally to the gross weight of 5,000 pounds (item 4). From this point, the line is followed vertically downward to 2,050 feet per minute (item 5), the rate of climb for a standard day at that altitude.

The standard temperature is found by entering the chart at the standard altitude and moving horizontally to the right until intersecting the standard temperature line (item 6). From this point, a line is followed vertically downward to read the standard temperature of nine degrees Fahrenheit (item 7).

The airplane's outside air temperature gauge is compared to the standard tem-

TWO-ENGINE CLIMB
STANDARD DAY (ISA)

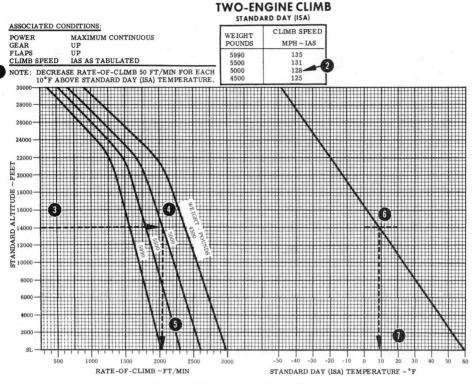

ASSOCIATED CONDITIONS:

POWER	MAXIMUM CONTINUOUS
GEAR	UP
FLAPS	UP
CLIMB SPEED	IAS AS TABULATED

1 NOTE: DECREASE RATE-OF-CLIMB 50 FT/MIN FOR EACH 10°F ABOVE STANDARD DAY (ISA) TEMPERATURE.

WEIGHT POUNDS	CLIMB SPEED MPH ~ IAS
5990	135
5500	131
5000	128
4500	125

Fig. 2-13. Two-Engine Climb Chart

perature. Since the thermometer reads 19° Fahrenheit, there is a +10° difference. The rate of climb is adjusted to 2,000 f.p.m. after reference to the note (item 1).

SINGLE-ENGINE CLIMB

The single-engine rate-of-climb chart, shown in figure 2-14, is also unique to multi-engine operations and provides some very important information. This chart is based on using maximum continuous power on the operative engine with the landing gear and flaps retracted while maintaining the specified airspeed (item 1). In addition, the inoperative engine's propeller is feathered rather than windmilling.

The dashed line in figure 2-14 shows the solution to a typical problem using the same conditions outlined for the two-engine climb. The single-engine climb rate is found by entering the chart at

14,000 feet (item 2), then moving horizontally to the gross weight of 5,000 pounds (item 3). From this point a line is followed vertically downward to 380 f.p.m. (item 4), the rate of climb for a standard day at that altitude.

The standard temperature and temperature difference are found in the same manner as the previous two-engine example by using items 5 and 6. In this case, the rate of climb is reduced by 25 f.p.m. to 355 f.p.m. Additional adjustments may be required if the airplane is being flown in other than a clean configuration (item 7).

Two other important figures that can be obtained from this chart or from the listed performance data are the single-engine service ceiling and the single-engine absolute ceiling. The *single-engine service ceiling* is the maximum altitude at which the airplane can produce a 50

PERFORMANCE CONSIDERATIONS

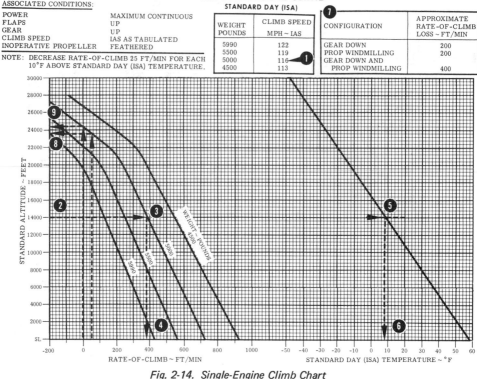

Fig. 2-14. Single-Engine Climb Chart

f.p.m. rate of climb with the critical engine (if appropriate) inoperative.

This service ceiling can be found on the chart by proceeding vertically upward on the 50 f.p.m. rate-of-climb line to the airplane's gross weight line and reading the service ceiling of 23,600 feet (item 8) to the left.

The *single-engine absolute ceiling* is the altitude at which the airplane will no longer climb with one engine inoperative. This important altitude may be determined by moving vertically upward on the zero f.p.m. line to the intersection of the airplane's gross weight line (item 9). At a gross weight of 5,000 pounds, the single-engine absolute ceiling is approximately 24,400 feet.

CRUISE PERFORMANCE CHARTS

The cruise performance charts in the pilot's operating handbook are used to determine power settings, fuel consumption, true airspeed, and range. It is quite common for more than one of these values to be presented on a single chart, as shown in figure 2-15.

From this chart, the pilot is able to determine the proper engine speed, manifold pressure, fuel flow per engine, and true airspeed. These charts are presented for various power settings such as 45, 55, and 65 percent horsepower. For example, if the airplane is being flown at 65 percent maximum continuous power at 14,000 feet and the outside air temperature is -13° Celsius, the following information can be determined.

Engine speed .... 2,500 r.p.m.
Manifold pressure ..... 30.4 in. Hg
Fuel flow per engine ... 18.6 g.p.h.
True airspeed .... 200 kts.

RANGE PROFILE

The range profile chart utilizes pressure altitude and power to determine the true

CRUISE POWER SETTINGS

65% MAXIMUM CONTINUOUS POWER (OR FULL THROTTLE)

PRESS ALT.	ISA-36°F (-20°C)							STANDARD DAY (ISA)							ISA +36°F (+20°C)						
	OAT	ENGINE SPEED	MAN. PRESS	FUEL FLOW PER ENGINE		TAS		OAT	ENGINE SPEED	MAN. PRESS	FUEL FLOW PER ENGINE		TAS		OAT	ENGINE SPEED	MAN PRESS	FUEL FLOW PER ENGINE		TAS	
FEET	°C	RPM	IN HG	PPH	GPH	KTS	MPH	°C	RPM	IN HG	PPH	GPH	KTS	MPH	°C	RPM	IN HG	PPH	GPH	KTS	MPH
SL	-5	2500	28.9	112	18.6	173	199	15	2500	29.8	112	18.6	177	204	35	2500	30.6	112	18.6	180	207
2000	-9	2500	28.9	112	18.6	176	203	11	2500	29.8	112	18.6	180	207	31	2500	20.7	112	18.6	183	211
4000	-13	2500	29.0	112	18.6	179	206	7	2500	29.8	112	18.6	183	211	27	2500	30.9	112	18.6	186	214
6000	-17	2500	29.0	112	18.6	182	209	3	2500	29.9	112	18.6	186	214	23	2500	31.0	112	18.6	190	219
8000	-21	2500	29.2	112	18.6	185	213	-1	2500	30.0	112	18.6	189	218	19	2500	31.1	112	18.6	193	222
10000	-25	2500	29.2	112	18.6	188	216	-5	2500	30.2	112	18.6	193	222	15	2500	31.2	112	18.6	197	227
12000	-29	2500	29.2	112	18.6	192		-9	2500	30.3	112	18.6	196	226	11	2500	31.4	112	18.6	200	230
14000	-33	2500	29.2	112	18.6	195	224	-13	2500	30.4	112	18.6	200	230	7	2500	31.5	112	18.6	204	235
16000	-37	2500	29.3	112	18.6	199	229	-17	2500	30.5	112	18.6	204	235	3	2500	31.6	112	18.6	208	239
18000	-41	2500	29.3	112	18.6	202	233	-21	2500	30.6	112	18.6	207	238	-1	2500	31.7	112	18.6	212	244
20000	-44	2500	29.4	112	18.6	206	237	-24	2500	30.6	112	18.6	211	243	-4	2500	31.8	112	18.6	216	249
22000	-48	2500	29.5	112	18.6	211	243	-28	2500	30.8	112	18.6	216	249	-8	2500	32.0	112	18.6	221	254
24000	-53	2500	29.8	112	18.6	215	247	-33	2500	31.1	112	18.6	220	253	-13	2500	32.0	111	18.5	224	258
26000	-57	2500	30.0	112	18.6	219	252	-37	2500	31.3	112	18.6	225	259	-17	2500	32.0	109	18.2	227	261
28000	-61	2500	29.9	110	18.3	222	256	-41	2500	29.9	105	17.5	223	257	-21	2500	29.9	100	16.7	223	257
30000	-64	2500	26.4	94	15.7	210	242	-44	2500	26.4	91	15.1	210	242	-24	2500	26.4	88	14.7	206	237

NOTES:
1. FULL THROTTLE MANIFOLD PRESSURE SETTINGS ARE APPROXIMATE.
2. ACTUAL BRAKE HORSEPOWER FOR FULL THROTTLE CONDITIONS (ABOVE CRITICAL ALTITUDE) MAY BE DETERMINED BY ENTERING THE GRAPH OF FUEL FLOW VS. BRAKE HORSEPOWER AT THE APPROPRIATE FUEL FLOW.
3. SHADED AREA REPRESENTS OPERATION WITH FULL THROTTLE.

Fig. 2-15. Cruise Power Settings

airspeed and range in nautical miles. The chart in figure 2-16 provides the range available with three different fuel tank configurations. This chart will be used to determine approximate KTAS and range in nautical miles under the following conditions.

Pressure altitude ...... 10,000 ft.
Brake horsepower............65%
Fuel .... 978 lbs.

The chart is entered from the left margin at pressure altitude of 10,000 feet (item 1). A line is followed horizontally until it reaches the diagonal 65 percent BHP line (item 2). The approximate true airspeed is read at this intersection. The approximate range of 970 n.m. (item 3) is read at the bottom of the chart on the scale for a 978-pound fuel load.

This particular range profile chart's information includes fuel required for start, taxi, takeoff, cruise climb to altitude, cruise, descent and 45 minutes reserve fuel at 45 percent power. The distances shown are the sum of the distances to climb, cruise, and descend.

NORMAL LANDING DISTANCE CHARTS

Charts also are supplied to determine the distance required to stop after landing. The normal landing distance chart presented in figure 2-17 provides landing information for a normal ground roll and the total distance to clear a 50-foot obstacle using different landing gross weights, speeds, pressure altitudes, and temperatures.

Under the listed conditions, the expected landing ground roll and total distance to clear a 50-foot obstacle are 500 feet and 1,650 feet, respectively.

Gross weight .... 4,600 lbs.
Speed at obstacle ...... 86 KIAS

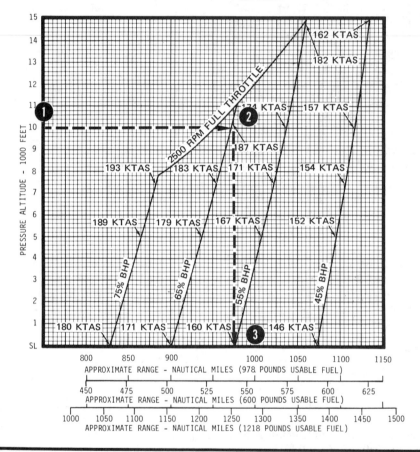

Fig. 2-16. Range Profile Chart

Temperature .... 20°C
Pressure altitude .... 2,000 ft.

The specified conditions of a hard-surfaced, level, dry runway; 35° flaps; and maximum braking effort are also included. Since different runway conditions require certain adjustments, various allowances are included in the note section.

STALLING SPEED CHARTS

Power-off stalling speeds vary with different flap configurations, gross weights, and bank angles. The power-off stalling speeds appropriate to these factors can be determined from the stalling speed versus weight and stalling speed versus angle-of-bank charts.

NORMAL LANDING DISTANCE

CONDITIONS:
1. Throttles - IDLE.
2. Landing Gear - DOWN.
3. Wing Flaps - 35°.
4. Cowl Flaps - CLOSE.
5. Level, Hard Surface Runway.
6. Maximum Braking Effort.

NOTE:
1. Increase distance by 25% of ground run for operation on firm sod runway.
2. If necessary to land with wing flaps UP, the approach speed should be increased above the normal approach speed by 12 knots. Expect total landing distance to increase by 35%.
3. Decrease total distances by 3% for each 4 knots headwind. For operations with tailwinds up to 10 knots, increase total distances by 5% for each 2 knots wind.

WEIGHT-POUNDS	SPEED AT 50-FOOT OBSTACLE KIAS	PRESSURE ALTITUDE - FEET	20°C (68°F)		30°C (86°F)		40°C (104°F)	
			GROUND ROLL - FEET	TOTAL DISTANCE TO CLEAR 50-FOOT OBSTACLE	GROUND ROLL - FEET	TOTAL DISTANCE TO CLEAR 50-FOOT OBSTACLE	GROUND ROLL - FEET	TOTAL DISTANCE TO CLEAR 50-FOOT OBSTACLE
5400	93	Sea Level	660	1810	680	1830	700	1850
		1000	680	1830	700	1850	730	1880
		2000	710	1860	730	1880	750	1900
		3000	730	1880	760	1910	780	1930
		4000	760	1910	780	1930	810	1960
		5000	790	1940	810	1960	840	1990
		6000	820	1970	850	2000	870	2020
		7000	850	2000	880	2030	910	2060
		8000	880	2030	910	2060	940	2090
		9000	920	2070	950	2100	980	2130
		10,000	950	2100	980	2130	1020	2170
5000	89	Sea Level	550	1700	570	1720	590	1740
		1000	570	1720	590	1740	610	1760
		2000	600	1750	620	1770	640	1790
		3000	620	1770	640	1790	660	1810
		4000	640	1790	660	1810	680	1830
		5000	670	1820	690	1840	710	1860
		6000	690	1840	710	1860	740	1890
		7000	720	1870	740	1890	770	1920
		8000	750	1900	770	1920	800	1950
		9000	770	1920	800	1950	830	1980
		10,000	800	1950	830	1980	860	2010
4600	86	Sea Level	460	1610	480	1630	490	1640
		1000	480	1630	500	1650	510	1660
		2000	500	1650	510	1660	530	1680
		3000	520	1670	530	1680	550	1700
		4000	530	1680	550	1700	570	1720
		5000	550	1700	570	1720	590	1740
		6000	580	1730	600	1750	610	1760
		7000	600	1750	620	1770	640	1790
		8000	620	1770	640	1790	660	1810
		9000	650	1800	670	1820	690	1840
		10,000	670	1820	690	1840	720	1870
4200	82	Sea Level	380	1530	390	1540	410	1560
		1000	390	1540	410	1560	420	1570
		2000	410	1560	420	1570	440	1590
		3000	420	1570	440	1590	450	1600
		4000	440	1590	450	1600	470	1620
		5000	460	1610	470	1620	490	1640
		6000	470	1620	490	1640	500	1650
		7000	490	1640	510	1660	520	1670
		8000	510	1660	530	1680	540	1690
		9000	530	1680	550	1700	560	1710
		10,000	550	1700	570	1720	590	1740

Fig. 2-17. Normal Landing Distance Chart

GROSS WEIGHT

Figure 2-18 shows the power-off, level flight stalling speed at various gross weights with the gear extended. The upper line represents the stalling speed with the flaps retracted. Since the stalling speed on the chart is given in calibrated airspeed, the pilot must use the airspeed correction table to determine the appropriate indicated airspeed.

The dashed lines in figure 2-18 represent the solution to a typical problem under the following conditions.

Power .... Off
Gross weight .... 4,200 lbs.
Landing gear .... Extended

The appropriate stalling speed with flaps retracted is 76 m.p.h. CAS (item 1).

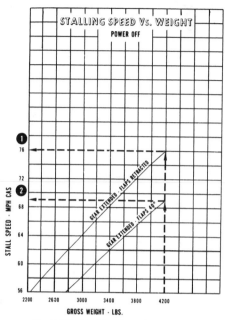

Fig. 2-18. Stalling Speed vs. Weight

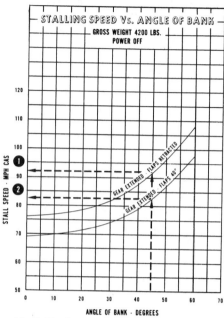

Fig. 2-19. Stalling Speed vs. Angle of Bank

Extension of 40° of flaps decreases the stalling speed to about 69 m.p.h. CAS (item 2).

ANGLE OF BANK

Figure 2-19 illustrates the stalling speeds with the gear extended at various angles of bank. The top line represents an airplane with the flaps retracted and the lower line represents one with the flaps extended. The dashed lines represent the solution to a problem under the listed conditions.

Power . . . . Off
Gross weight . . . . 4,200 lbs.
Gear . . . . Extended

The appropriate stalling speed with flaps retracted is approximately 92 m.p.h. CAS (item 1). Extension of 40° of flaps decreases the stalling speed to about 83 m.p.h. CAS (item 2).

chapter 3

ENGINE-OUT OPERATIONS

INTRODUCTION

The obvious advantage of the multi-engine airplane is that the failure of an engine leaves the pilot with more alternatives than his counterpart in the single-engine airplane. However, the exact parameters of those alternatives are more difficult to define. This chapter provides a framework for determining the performance that can be expected following an engine failure and explains the aerodynamic factors and piloting techniques involved with single-engine flight.

SECTION A—AERODYNAMICS

When an engine fails, the greatest overall performance loss results from a 50 percent reduction in available horsepower. However, the total loss of *climb performance* when one engine fails is approximately 80 percent for most light, conventional, twin-engine airplanes. The additional 30 percent loss results from asymmetrical thrust and drag and the control responses necessary to compensate for these factors.

Due to this performance loss, the multi-engine pilot must not assume his airplane will climb with one engine inoperative. Although aircraft certified under FAR Part 23 are required to meet certain performance and handling criteria, many light twin-engine airplanes are not required to demonstrate climbing ability during single-engine operations. The regulation requires a positive engine-out rate of climb at 5,000 feet density altitude only for those multi-engine airplanes weighing more than 6,000 pounds and/or having a stalling speed (V_{SO}) greater than 61 knots. If the airplane weighs 6,000 pounds or less and has a stalling speed of 61 knots or less, a specific, *positive* engine-out rate of climb is not required. However, the manufacturer must determine what the engine-out climb performance is at 5,000 feet with the critical engine inoperative and its propeller in the minimum drag configuration.

CRITICAL ENGINE

The term *critical engine* refers to the engine whose failure most adversely affects the performance or handling characteristics of the airplane. Consideration of the critical engine is most significant in situations where the airplane is operating at low speeds with a high power setting. In these high angle of attack attitudes, the descending blade of each propeller is producing more thrust than the ascending blade. The unequal thrust vector can be related to the "moment" presented in weight and balance. The longitudinal axis of the airplane is considered the datum for this discussion, and each of the descending propeller blades is given an "arm." Thus, the thrust from each engine may be measured as a "moment arm," as illustrated in figure 3-1.

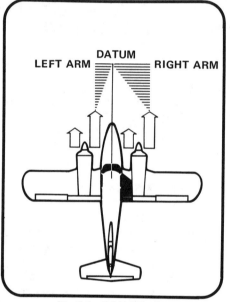

Fig. 3-1. Critical Engine

If the left engine failed, directional control would be affected more than if the right engine became inoperative. The larger moment arm associated with the right engine would have a greater influence than that of the left engine, as shown in figure 3-2. Therefore, in conventional multi-engine airplanes, the left engine is the critical engine.

MINIMUM CONTROL SPEED

V_{MC} is the minimum controllable airspeed with the critical engine (if applicable) inoperative and the other engine producing takeoff power. The propeller on the inoperative engine must be either windmilling at low pitch or feathered if the airplane is equipped with an automatic feathering device. In addition, V_{MC} is determined at gross weight with the center of gravity at the aft limit, landing gear retracted, and the flaps in the takeoff position. The manufacturer's published minimum control speed and actual V_{MC} may vary as the power on the noncritical engine changes. Figure 3-3 illustrates that at a constant altitude there are an infinite number of minimum controllable airspeeds as the power is varied. In addition, normally aspirated engines lose efficiency as altitude increases and are unable to develop 100 percent rated sea level power. This power loss also causes actual V_{MC} to decrease.

While actual V_{MC} is decreasing with altitude, it must be remembered that the calibrated stalling speed remains the same. Figure 3-4 illustrates the effect of altitude on actual V_{MC} and shows that stalling speed and V_{MC} eventually converge. Therefore, the pilot should not assume that he may safely fly below published V_{MC} even though he is flying at a high density altitude.

STABILITY AND CONTROL

The primary concern after engine failure is to keep the aircraft controllable and stabilize the attitude for increased performance. Control effectiveness in any flight situation is dependent upon the velocity of the airflow over the control surface. At airspeeds below V_{MC}, full control deflection does not provide sufficient force to overcome the yawing and rolling tendencies induced by failure of the critical engine.

INDUCED AIRFLOW

When either engine fails, the induced flow from propeller slipstream is lost and

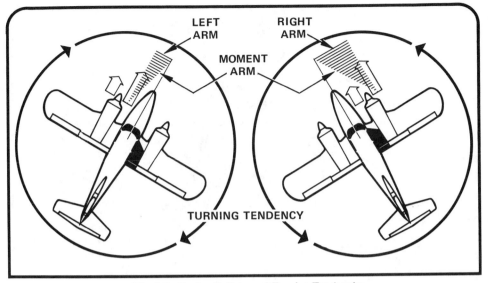

Fig. 3-2. Engine Failure and Turning Tendencies

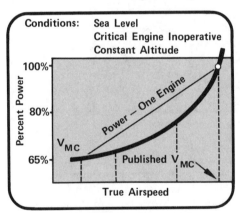

Fig. 3-3. Percent Power and Minimum Control Speed

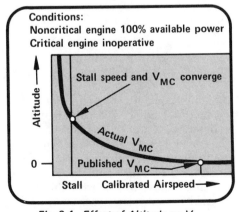

Fig. 3-4. Effect of Altitude on V_{MC}

total lift on that wing is decreased. Without corrective action, the airplane will roll in the direction of the inoperative engine. When this occurs, some airflow also is blocked by the fuselage since the flight path is no longer parallel to the longitudinal axis, as shown in figure 3-5.

ASYMMETRICAL THRUST AND DRAG

The asymmetrical thrust and drag created by loss of an engine must be counteracted with the aircraft flight controls, which have a maximum limit of deflection and effectiveness. The effectiveness of control surfaces decreases with airspeed. Therefore, at any given power setting above idle, there is a minimum airspeed at which the aerodynamic action on the flight controls will counteract yaw and roll toward the inoperative engine. At any airspeed below V_{MC}, this yaw and roll cannot be stopped unless power is reduced on the operative engine to reduce asymmetrical thrust.

Considerable control pressures are necessary to counter the rolling and yawing moments encountered during flight with

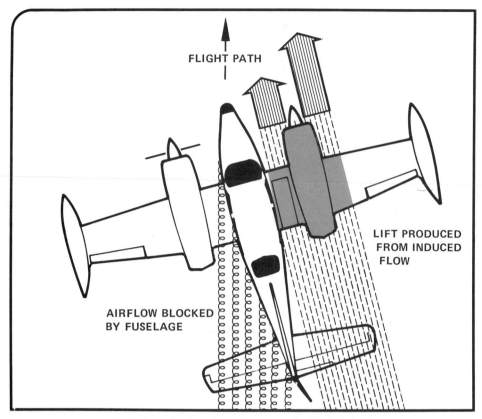

Fig. 3-5. Rolling Tendency Due to Lack of Induced Flow

one engine. However, rudder deflection can be minimized if the airplane is banked three to five degrees toward the operative engine. In this configuration, the high wing produces a lift vector which acts to relieve the rudder forces required to maintain straight flight.

When a control surface, such as the ailerons or the rudder, is displaced from the neutral position, a proportional amount of drag is created. Figure 3-6 illustrates the parasite drag created by the inoperative engine and the induced drag caused by the displacement of control surfaces. The thrust being produced by the operating engine is also shown.

The windmilling propeller of the "failed" engine creates a substantial amount of the total drag encountered during stabilized single-engine flight. Figure 3-7 shows the relationship of the windmilling propeller and stationary propeller to blade angle and drag created. These thrust/drag comparisons illustrate the reason for feathering the propeller of the inoperative engine if it cannot be restarted immediately.

LOADING

Minimum control speed also is affected by aircraft loading. The published V_{MC} is determined under controlled conditions, and is accurate only when those conditions are duplicated. This would require use of a new airplane, loaded to maximum gross weight with the center of gravity at the aft limit, operating in standard atmospheric conditions.

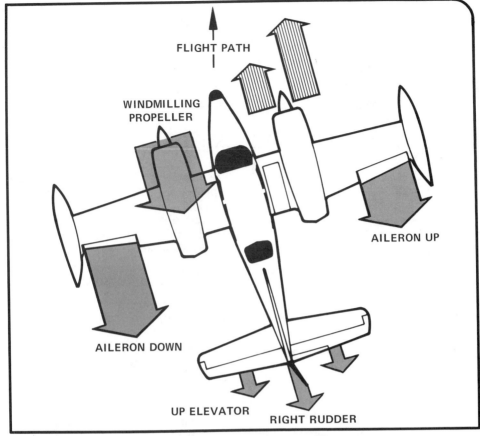

Fig. 3-6. Asymmetrical Thrust and Drag

As a rule of thumb, the actual V_{MC} will be lower if the airplane is at less than gross weight and the CG is forward of the aft limit. Conversely, the V_{MC} will be much *higher* if the airplane is loaded heavier than certified gross weight or aft of the rear CG limit.

Situations should be avoided where loading could affect control during engine-out operations. In airplanes where wing-mounted tanks are located outboard of the engines, fuel management should not allow for a heavy fuel load on the side of the critical engine and a light fuel load on the other side. Loading should always follow the manufacturer's recommendations.

COUNTERROTATING ENGINES

When an airplane is equipped with counterrotating propellers, neither engine is considered critical. As illustrated in figure 3-8, asymmetrical thrust is equal,

Fig. 3-7. Propeller Drag Contribution

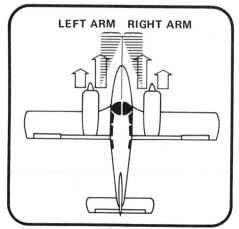

LEFT ARM   RIGHT ARM

*Fig. 3-8. Asymmetrical Loading with
Counterrotating Engines*

regardless of which engine is inoperative. Turning tendencies are still very apparent, but lack the severity of those associated with the critical engine failure of a conventional twin.

ENGINE-OUT V-SPEEDS

An engine failure in a twin usually means that the best climb performance available is only marginal when compared to the performance with both engines operating. Climb airspeeds are published by the manufacturer for best rate and best angle during single-engine operation. These airspeeds are referred to as V_{YSE} and V_{XSE}, respectively. In addition, some manufacturers establish a minimum speed for intentionally rendering one engine inoperative. This speed, which is applicable to training activities, is generally called V_{SSE}.

BEST RATE OF CLIMB—SINGLE ENGINE

V_{YSE} is the speed which produces the greatest gain in altitude in a given amount of time with one engine inoperative. This airspeed normally is used if altitude is a prime consideration after engine failure. If engine failure occurs above the airplane's single-engine service ceiling, this airspeed produces the minimum descent rate with the operative engine at maximum continuous power.

BEST ANGLE OF CLIMB—SINGLE ENGINE

V_{XSE} is the engine-out best angle-of-climb airspeed. This speed is used for obstruction clearance with one engine inoperative. In most cases, V_{XSE} is a somewhat higher airspeed than the twin-engine best angle-of-climb speed (V_X).

SINGLE-ENGINE CEILINGS

The operating altitudes of multi-engine airplanes are lowered considerably during single-engine flight. The engine loss reduces total thrust available and corresponding reductions of *service ceiling* and *absolute ceiling* result.

SINGLE-ENGINE SERVICE CEILING

The single-engine service ceiling is the maximum density altitude at which the single-engine best rate-of-climb airspeed (V_{YSE}) will produce a 50 f.p.m. rate of climb. The ability to climb 50 f.p.m. in calm air is necessary to maintain *level flight* for long periods in turbulent air. This ceiling assumes the airplane is at gross weight in the clean configuration, the critical engine (if appropriate) inoperative, and the propeller feathered. In comparison, the multi-engine service ceiling is the density altitude at which the best rate-of-climb airspeed (V_Y) will produce a 100 f.p.m. rate of climb at gross weight in the clean configuration.

SINGLE-ENGINE ABSOLUTE CEILING

The single-engine absolute ceiling is the maximum density altitude the airplane is capable of attaining or maintaining. This ceiling assumes the airplane is at gross weight in the clean configuration, the critical engine (if appropriate) inoperative, and the propeller feathered. This is also the density altitude at which V_{XSE} and V_{YSE} are the same airspeed.

Figure 3-9 illustrates an engine failure at a cruising altitude above the single-

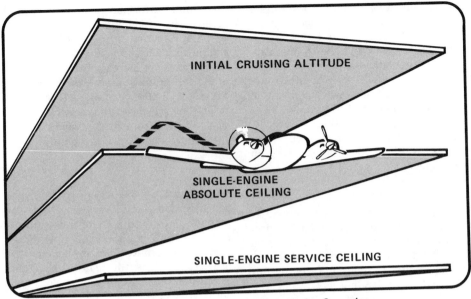

Fig. 3-9. Altitude Loss During Single-Engine Operation

engine absolute ceiling. In this situation, the aircraft will descend gradually (drift down) to the density altitude equivalent of the single-engine absolute ceiling appropriate to the existing gross weight. In turbulent air, the airplane may not be capable of maintaining the single-engine absolute ceiling and may continue to descend to the single-engine service ceiling or lower.

SINGLE-ENGINE CLIMB

Climb performance is dependent upon the ratio of thrust to drag. If drag exceeds thrust, climb is not possible and the best rate-of-climb speed will provide the least rate of descent. Figure 3-10 depicts a typical drag curve with available thrust when one engine is inoperative. Any thrust and airspeed combination that falls within the shaded area represents a positive rate of climb. Conversely, any point outside the shaded area will produce a descent. This graph also illustrates the thrust available on the same airplane at 15,000 feet. At that altitude, drag exceeds thrust and a positive rate of climb cannot be established.

Drag is a major factor in the amount of excess thrust available. Any increase in drag, whether parasite or induced, must be balanced by the use of additional thrust. Any use of excess thrust to counteract drag is thrust which cannot be used for the climb. Since the extension of the landing gear and/or flaps increases parasite drag, the maximum amount of excess thrust is available in the clean configuration. In most light and medium twin-engine airplanes, the extension of the landing gear or flaps may increase drag in excess of the available thrust causing a descent.

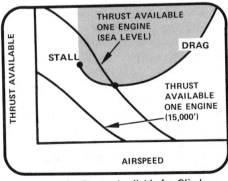

Fig. 3-10. Thrust Available for Climb

Drag also increases because of the rudder and aileron deflections necessary to maintain straight flight and the airflow restriction caused by the inoperative engine's propeller. An increase in airspeed also increases drag. Therefore, any speed above that necessary to maintain level flight or above V_{YSE} during a climb requires excess thrust and decreases the airplane's performance. All of this results in a dramatic decrease in performance.

It is important that the pilot be familiar with the correct order for drag reduction following an engine failure. Normally, a windmilling propeller contributes the greatest amount of drag, followed by full flaps, extended landing gear, and the control deflections required to stop the airplane from turning. Since it is considered unwise to immediately feather an engine before it has been positively identified, drag is normally reduced by first retracting flaps and gear. Next, the failed engine is identified and the propeller is feathered. However, the specific order of drag reduction may vary between types of twin-engine airplanes, so the manufacturer's recommendations should be followed. During training, it is beneficial to use the vertical velocity indicator to compare the relative engine-out performance loss associated with a windmilling propeller, full flaps, and extended landing gear.

Performance will be decreased still further by any increase in density altitude. Density altitude will affect the single-engine climb rate as it affects the twin-engine climb rate, but the results are more critical during engine-out operations. For example, the single-engine climb rate normally is very small for most light multi-engine airplanes. Therefore, any decrease in this performance because of higher density altitude will quickly result in a negligible climb rate or a possible descent.

The climb performance can be improved greatly by reducing operating gross weights. As an example, a typical multi-engine airplane's sea level single-engine climb rate may increase from 230 f.p.m. at 4,000 pounds gross weight to 420 f.p.m. at 3,400 pounds. At the same time, the single-engine service ceiling may increase from 5,200 feet to 10,000 feet under standard atmospheric conditions.

With regard to the above performance considerations, it is evident that the takeoff and climb are the most critical phases of all multi-engine operations. During this time, the airplane is the heaviest it will be throughout the flight. Therefore, the single-engine rate of climb and service ceiling are the lowest.

Turns, except to avoid obstructions, should be limited during a single-engine climb until the airplane has reached a safe altitude to return to the airport. Even a perfectly coordinated turn increases induced drag which, in turn, increases the amount of thrust required to maintain altitude. This results in less excess thrust for climb. If a turn is necessary, the smallest bank angle possible for the existing conditions should be used. To illustrate this point, figure 3-11 shows that, at a constant airspeed, a 15° bank increases the induced drag by approximately seven percent while a 30° bank results in a 33 percent increase.

Because of the increased drag and decreased control effectiveness, it is recommended that the maximum bank angle of 15° be used during single-engine maneuvering and then only after a safe maneuvering altitude is attained. The 15° bank should be maximum because of the rapid drag increase associated with higher bank angles. As illustrated, a five degree increase from 15° to 20° of bank nearly doubles the percentage increase in induced drag.

BANK ANGLE, DEGREES	LOAD FACTOR	PERCENT INCREASE IN STALL SPEED	PERCENT INCREASE IN INDUCED DRAG (AT CONSTANT VELOCITY)
0	1.0000	0	0
5	1.0038	0.2	0.8
10	1.0154	0.7	3.1
15	1.0353	1.7	7.2
20	1.0642	3.2	13.3
25	1.1034	5.0	21.7
30	1.1547	7.5	33.3
35	1.2208	10.5	49.0
40	1.3054	14.3	70.4
45	1.4142	18.9	100.0
60	2.0000	41.4	300.0

Fig. 3-11. Bank Angle and Induced Drag

The entire discussion of asymmetrical thrust, V_{MC}, and single-engine climbs has pointed out that takeoff and initial climb are the most critical phases of multi-engine operations. The pilot must continually analyze his aircraft's performance in order to know what single-engine performance can be expected in the event of engine failure or partial power loss.

SECTION B—PROCEDURES AND MANEUVERS

As discussed in the previous section, the aerodynamic factors affecting flight with one engine inoperative are significant and critical. This section will apply these aerodynamic relationships to the practical aspects of engine-out operations, beginning with engine shutdown procedures and followed by in-flight maneuvers.

ENGINE SHUTDOWN

The decision to shut down a failing engine is a matter of pilot judgment, based on the circumstances involved at that particular time. If an engine has failed completely, it is obvious that it should be shut down and the propeller feathered to reduce drag. However, the pilot should seriously consider continued use of an engine that is producing partial power. Even though maximum power is not available, a reduced power output is better than none.

IDENTIFYING THE INOPERATIVE ENGINE

After an engine has failed, the pilot's primary concern is to maintain control of the airplane and identify the inoperative engine. The following discussion pertains to the techniques of identifying the failed engine. Actual shutdown procedures will be discussed later in this chapter.

YAW AND ROLL

The first indication of an engine failure is a pronounced yaw and roll, which always occurs in the direction of the inoperative engine. As these conditions develop, the pilot must apply rudder to maintain a constant heading. The control application provides a second indication of the inoperative engine because the foot which is not applying rudder pressure is on the same side as the failed engine. The memory aid, "idle foot, idle engine," often is used in multi-engine

training to identify a failed engine. For example, if the airplane begins to yaw to the right, the pilot must apply left rudder to maintain directional control. Therefore, his right foot is not applying rudder pressure, which corresponds to the failed right engine.

ENGINE INSTRUMENTS

Certain engine instruments also may aid the pilot in identifying the failed engine. Specifically, the fuel-flow and fuel-pressure gauges should be observed to determine if the failure was caused by fuel starvation. In addition, the EGT and cylinder head temperatures may be decreasing or lower than those of the operating engine. Figure 3-12 lists important indications of a failed engine.

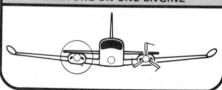

1. PRONOUNCED YAWING AND ROLLING TENDENCY
2. HEAVY RUDDER PRESSURE REQUIRED FOR DIRECTIONAL CONTROL
3. LOSS IN FUEL FLOW ON ONE ENGINE
4. COOLER CYLINDER HEAD TEMPERATURE ON ONE ENGINE

Fig. 3-12. Indications of a Failed Engine

ENGINE POWER CONTROLS

At the same time the pilot is regaining control of the airplane and checking the engine instruments, the mixtures are advanced to *full rich*, the propellers are moved to *high r.p.m.*, and the throttles are advanced to *maximum power*. This procedure guarantees that the operating engine is producing maximum power, regardless of which engine is inoperative. During this application of power, special attention must be given to directional control, because as the power is increased, the amount of required rudder also will increase. In addition, as directional control is maintained, the airspeed must be no lower than the single-engine best rate-of-climb airspeed (V_{YSE}).

VERIFICATION

After the inoperative engine has been identified, it is vital to *verify* that the correct analysis has been made. To verify the inoperative engine and safeguard against shutting down the operating engine, the pilot should retard the throttle on the *suspected* failed engine. If the correct engine has been selected there will be no change in airplane performance or the amount of rudder pressure required to counteract yaw. If the engine is developing partial power, the asymmetrical thrust will increase as the throttle is retarded. In this case, it may be desirable to keep the engine operating until a safe altitude is reached and the nature of the problem determined. However, if the incorrect engine has been

selected, the asymmetrical thrust will decrease, and the throttle must be advanced immediately to regain maximum engine power. Failure to first identify and then verify the failed engine before shutdown can have grave consequences, as depicted in figure 3-13.

ENGINE SHUTDOWN PROCEDURES

Since the engine shutdown and securing procedures may vary between each make and model of airplane, the appropriate pilot's operating handbook should be consulted for specific details. However, the basic procedures are the same for all piston engine airplanes. The expanded list of steps shown in figure 3-14 applies to all airplanes.

Items 1 through 11 should be committed to memory so they are available for immediate recall and action in the event of an engine failure. If time permits after the airplane is trimmed, the pilot should complete the entire printed engine-out checklist to verify all items have been completed. In addition, during this re-

Fig. 3-13. Failing to Verify the Failed Engine

ENGINE SHUTDOWN AND SECURING PROCEDURES

1. Maintain directional control by applying rudder to maintain a constant heading.
2. Maintain V_{YSE} as a minimum airspeed.
3. Apply maximum power by moving the mixtures, props, and throttles full forward.
4. Reduce the drag by retracting the flaps and landing gear.
5. Check auxiliary fuel boost pumps—ON.
6. Check that the fuel selector is in the proper position.
7. Identify the inoperative engine by using the "idle foot, idle engine" test.
8. Verify the inoperative engine by closing the appropriate throttle.
9. Feather the propeller by moving the propeller lever to the feather position.
10. Move the mixture control to idle cutoff.
11. Trim excess control pressures.
12. Secure the inoperative engine by using the following steps.
    A. Fuel selector—OFF
    B. Auxiliary boost pump—OFF
    C. Magneto switches—OFF
    D. Alternator—OFF
    E. Cowl Flap—CLOSED
13. Review checklist.

Fig. 3-14. Engine Shutdown Checklist

view, the inoperative engine should be secured and the prelanding checklist reviewed.

If the engine failure occurs during the takeoff or initial climb, it is obvious that single-engine performance is at its most critical level. In this condition, the maintenance of V_{YSE} (or V_{XSE} if obstacles are a factor), prompt identification of the inoperative engine, and propeller feathering are of prime importance. If the pretakeoff checklist has been followed correctly, the pilot can be sure that the fuel selectors are on the proper tanks, the boost pumps are on, the propeller controls are full forward, and the mixtures are set properly. Therefore, if the engine failure occurs on takeoff, only a quick review of these items is necessary prior to engine identification and propeller feathering. In this manner, optimum single-engine performance may be achieved in a minimum amount of time.

If an engine failure occurs during cruise, a prompt engine shutdown is not as critical. In this situation, the pilot normally has adequate time to analyze the problem and attempt to restore the engine's power. If the problem cannot be remedied, the engine should be shut down and the propeller feathered to conserve altitude.

ENGINE SHUTDOWN RAMIFICATIONS

In addition to the shutdown of the inoperative engine, the pilot must give close attention to the operating engine from two standpoints. First, the combination of reduced airspeed and additional power demanded from the engine may cause overheating problems. Therefore, the oil temperature, oil pressure, and cylinder head temperature must be monitored and maintained in the normal operating ranges. If necessary, the cowl flaps should be opened and the mixture enriched to aid in engine temperature reduction. Second, single-engine flight also creates single alternator operation, which requires an appropriate reduction in electrical load. In addition, other systems such as hydraulics and pneumatics may have greatly reduced capabilities or become completely inoperative.

PROPELLER UNFEATHERING AND ENGINE RESTART

A common occurrence during multi-engine flight training is the propeller unfeathering and engine restart procedure. Figure 3-15 shows a typical checklist used for this procedure. It should be noted that item 6 calls for use of the engine starter to begin propeller rotation. This is necessary to create oil pressure from the propeller governor, which begins to move the propeller blades from high pitch (feather) to low pitch. The starter can be disengaged as the blades move out of the feather position, because the airflow passing over the blades will continue the rotation. Once the engine starts, the power should be kept to a minimum until the cylinder head and oil temperatures are within the normal operating ranges. This is important because the use of high power settings on a cold engine can result in engine damage.

RESTARTING PROCEDURES
1. Magneto Switches—ON
2. Fuel Selector—MAIN TANK
3. Throttle—FORWARD approximately one inch
4. Mixture—AS REQUIRED for flight altitude
5. Propeller—FORWARD of detent
6. Starter Button—PRESS—RELEASE when engine fires
7. Mixture—AS REQUIRED
8. Power—INCREASE after cylinder head temperature is adequate
9. Cowl Flap—AS REQUIRED
10. Alternator—ON

Fig. 3-15. In-Flight Engine Restart Procedure

If an engine is equipped with *unfeathering accumulators*, it is not necessary to use the starter to begin propeller rotation. The accumulator provides either hydraulic or pneumatic pressure to the feathering mechanism, which forces the blades out of the feather position. As the blades move from feather towards low pitch, the propellers gain sufficient blade angle to begin rotation because of the airflow. The propeller accumulator usually is activated by moving the appropriate propeller control lever full forward to the high r.p.m. setting.

ENGINE-OUT MANEUVERS

As previously discussed, the competent multi-engine pilot should be prepared for an engine failure during all phases of flight. Although the possibilities of an actual engine failure are somewhat remote, the pilot should always have a plan of action in the event of such an occurrence.

TAKEOFF

If the engine failure occurs during the takeoff ground run, the airplane will immediately turn in the direction of the failed engine. If this condition develops below the single-engine minimum control airspeed, the takeoff *must be discontinued*. In all twin-engine airplanes, this means closing both throttles immediately and applying braking as necessary to stop the airplane.

If the failure occurs when the airplane is airborne and sufficient runway remains for landing, the pilot should close both throttles and land, particularly if the landing gear is still extended. If the landing cannot be accomplished safely, a single-engine climb should be established to a safe maneuvering altitude, followed by a return to the airport for landing.

Under some circumstances, the pilot may elect to take off when the density altitude exceeds the airplane's single-engine service ceiling. When operating within this limitation, the pilot must not expect the airplane to have any single-engine climb capability. If engine failure occurs in this situation, the only alternative available is the prompt selection of a suitable off-airport landing area within the airplane's driftdown range. Under no circumstances can the pilot allow the airspeed to become lower than V_{MC}. The single-engine best rate-of-climb (V_{YSE}) airspeed should be maintained to provide the slowest rate of descent.

CLIMB

For normal multi-engine takeoffs, it is important to maintain V_Y during the initial climb. Any airspeed in excess of V_Y is not as valuable as the altitude that would have been gained since the drag of a failed engine will prevent efficient conversion of excess airspeed to altitude. If an engine failure occurs during climb at an airspeed of V_Y (after the landing gear and the flaps are retracted), the possibility of a sustained single-engine climb is greatly improved.

If an engine failure occurs during the climb and there are no obstacles to be cleared, the single-engine best rate-of-climb (V_{YSE}) should be maintained at the maximum continuous power setting. If the airspeed is below V_{YSE}, a momentary descent will be required to accelerate the airplane to the single-engine best rate-of-climb airspeed before the climb can be initiated. The pilots of light and medium twin-engine airplanes must realize that these airplanes have very narrow single-engine performance parameters. Any airspeed *above* or *below* V_{YSE} results in a reduced rate of climb.

To gain optimum single-engine performance during the climb, the airplane should be banked three to five degrees toward the operating engine. This technique reduces the amount of rudder deflection required to maintain directional control and, therefore reduces drag. The drag is reduced because the high wing produces additional lift which acts to assist rudder forces in turning the airplane away from the inoperative engine. Figure 3-16 shows that, in the case of the left engine out (position 1), a lift vector is created to the right because of the raised left wing.

The opposite is true if the airplane is banked toward the inoperative engine (position 2). In this situation, a lift vector is produced in the same direction as the yaw, requiring additional rudder deflection to overcome the turn vector. For this reason, the pilot must use extra care when turning in the direction of the inoperative engine. Turns in this direction can be made safely if the pilot is aware of the aerodynamic forces involved and maintains a safe margin above V_{MC}.

ENROUTE

As a general rule, an engine failure during the enroute phase of flight is not as critical as one which occurs during takeoff or climb. The pilot should have ample time to analyze the reason for the failure, attempt a restart, or secure the engine if it cannot be restarted. Even if the situation is not critical, it is good practice to apply full power to the good engine to conserve altitude during the attempt to correct the engine failure. As with every engine failure, the mixtures should be moved to full rich, the props moved to high r.p.m., the boost pumps turned on, and the fuel tanks checked to be sure the tank in use has fuel. Even if the tank has fuel, it is a good practice to select another tank which has fuel, since the fuel line from the original tank may be blocked. These steps are important because the most frequent cause of an enroute engine failure is fuel starvation.

When single-engine operations become necessary, the original cruising altitude often is higher than the airplane's single-engine absolute or service ceiling. In this situation, the pilot must accept the fact that a descent is inevitable until the airplane reaches the absolute ceiling. During the descent, V_{YSE} airspeed should be used to obtain the minimum

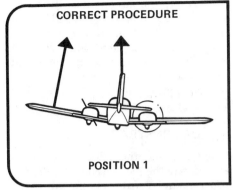
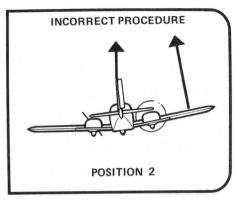

Fig. 3-16. Bank During Engine-Out Operations

rate of descent and conserve altitude as long as possible. The airspeed should never be reduced below V_{YSE} in an attempt to hold altitude.

Once it has been determined that an engine restart is not possible, the pilot should select the closest suitable airport in terms of time. Because of wind or other considerations, such as deteriorating weather, this may not be the closest airport in distance. Time is the prime factor if altitude cannot be maintained.

Although an extended period of flight is not recommended, it may be necessary to reach the destination or alternate airport. In this case, fuel from the wing tanks should be used evenly so the weight distribution on each side of the airplane remains equal. A fuel crossfeed is incorporated in the fuel system for this purpose and allows the pilot to select and use the fuel from the wing tanks on the side of the failed engine. The checklist should be studied carefully to determine the correct procedure for fuel crossfeed.

LANDING

An engine-out landing in a multi-engine airplane requires a well planned approach so that the initial attempt is successful. Generally, the only differences between a twin-engine approach and an engine-out approach are the size of the traffic pattern and the point at which the landing gear is extended.

A slightly larger traffic pattern may be flown to create shallower turns. The shallower turns provide better airplane control, better visibility and more time to plan for and monitor the approach.

Generally, the landing gear is not extended during the approach until the airplane is established at approach airspeed and the pilot is positively assured of reaching the desired runway. This timing is important since the extension of the landing gear adds sufficient drag to create a 300 to 500 f.p.m. rate of descent without a power reduction. However, it is important to allow sufficient time for a manual gear extension if the normal extension system fails. Some airplanes have hydraulic landing gear systems operated by only one hydraulic pump. If the hydraulic pump is installed on the inoperative engine, a manual extension is obviously required.

The wing flaps should be used as little as possible, preferably not at all until the landing gear is extended and the landing is assured. The pilot's operating handbook should be consulted to determine the maximum amount of flaps to be used during an engine-out landing.

ENGINE-OUT REJECTED LANDING

An engine-out rejected landing (go-around) is advisable only under the best conditions of weight, altitude, and temperature. In fact, if the density altitude at the airport and the aircraft's gross weight are very high, a single-engine go-around may be impossible. For these reasons, the single-engine approach should be planned carefully so a go-around is not required.

If it appears a go-around may be necessary, a decision should be made early in the approach to either land or reject the landing. To make this decision, the pilot should consider aircraft performance, terrain contour, and heights of obstacles in the vicinity of the airport. Then, he should establish a "go, no-go" altitude based on the altitude loss that occurs during the flap and gear retraction and the normal sink encountered during the transition to a single-engine climb. If a decision for a go-around is made before reaching this altitude, he should add full power, retract the flaps and landing gear, and climb at V_{YSE}. After this speed is established, the aircraft is retrimmed for single-engine flight if the pilot desires.

If, however, the aircraft has descended below the go, no-go altitude, the pilot should consider himself *committed to land*. Under certain conditions, the pilot may be better off to land on the side of the runway, a parallel taxiway, or even the grass next to the runway, rather than to attempt a go-around.

V_{MC} DEMONSTRATION

During training, the pilot will learn to demonstrate the recognition, effects, and proper recovery from attempted single-engine flight below V_{MC}. The procedure is illustrated in figure 3-17.

The purpose of the maneuver is to demonstrate that control cannot be maintained below the engine-out minimum control airspeed. The demonstration is performed in the clean configuration with one engine set to takeoff power and the other idling with the propeller windmilling. The speed is decreased slowly by increasing the pitch attitude until rudder control will no longer prevent the airplane from turning or banking in the direction of the inoperative engine. The demonstration should be terminated immediately if a stall

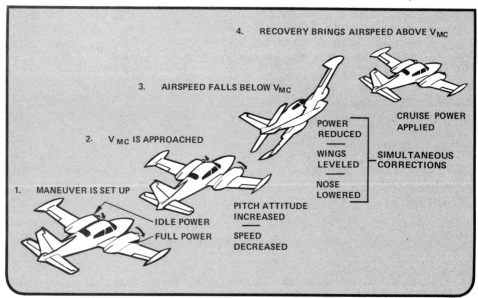

Fig. 3-17. V_{MC} Demonstration

indication is received prior to an indication of V_{MC}. At high density altitudes, a stall can occur prior to V_{MC}, resulting in a sudden loss of all control.

When the turning and rolling tendencies can no longer be overcome by control deflection, the power on the operative engine should be reduced to idle to decrease the asymmetrical thrust. Then, the attitude should be lowered to increase the airspeed above V_{MC}. Once control is regained and the airspeed is at or above V_{XSE}, power may be reapplied to the operative engine to terminate the demonstration.

WORKBOOK EXERCISES

INTRODUCTION

The Workbook Exercises are designed to complement the Multi-Engine Manual and the audiovisual presentations. Each exercise is correlated with a specific textbook chapter and section. For example, Exercise 1A applies to textbook Chapter 1, Section A.

The workbook contains multiple choice, true/false, matching, and completion exercises. To answer the multiple choice questions, circle the number of the correct choice. Fill in the appropriate blanks to answer the other questions. Further instructions may appear at the beginning of a section or within the body of an individual exercise, when necessary. The answers to all of the exercises are grouped at the back of the manual following the Pilot Briefing section.

CHAPTER 1—MULTI-ENGINE OPERATIONS AND SYSTEMS

Exercise 1A—Procedures And Maneuvers

1. _____ (True, False) Asymmetrical loading of the propellers contributes to the left-turning tendency in conventional multi-engine airplanes.

2. _____ (True, False) Torque contributes to a rolling moment in the same direction as propeller rotation.

3. If a rapid power reduction is made on a slow final approach, a high sink rate might be experienced because

    1. P-factor is reduced.
    2. the cowl flaps are open.
    3. induced airflow is reduced.
    4. torque is eliminated.

4. The V-speed which produces the best rate of climb in a twin-engine airplane is termed

    1. V_X.
    2. V_Y.
    3. V_{XSE}.
    4. V_{YSE}.

5. _____ (True, False) During takeoff in a strong crosswind, power can be increased on the downwind engine to counteract the weathervaning tendency.

6. The altitude where V_X and V_Y converge is known as the _____ _____.

7. _____ (True, False) Turbocharging increases the service ceiling of an airplane by providing the engines with enough power to produce additional lift at higher altitudes.

Complete the exercise below by matching the terms on the right, with the corresponding V-speed designations on the left.

8. _____ V_A

9. _____ V_{FE}

10. _____ V_{MC}

11. _____ V_{NE}

12. _____ V_{XSE}

13. _____ V_{YSE}

14. _____ V_{LE}

15. _____ V_{S1}

16. _____ V_{SO}

17. _____ V_{NO}

18. _____ V_Y

19. _____ V_X

A. Maximum flap extended speed
B. Minimum control speed
C. Best single-engine angle-of-climb speed
D. Maneuvering speed
E. Never-exceed speed
F. Best multi-engine angle-of-climb speed
G. Maximum structural cruising speed
H. Best multi-engine rate-of-climb speed
I. Maximum landing gear extended speed
J. Stalling speed in landing configuration
K. Best single-engine rate-of-climb speed
L. Stalling speed in a specified configuration

Arrange the items on the right in the proper preflight planning sequence.

20. _____

21. _____

22. _____

23. _____

24. _____

A. Consideration of terrain and obstructions
B. Determination of the airplane's runway requirements
C. Selection of alternatives in the event of engine failure
D. Review of engine-out airspeeds
E. Determination of density altitude

25. _____ (True, False) After a pilot has become familiar with a multi-engine airplane and has gained several hours of multi-engine flight experience, it is not necessary for him to refer to every item on the printed checklist.

26. _____ (True, False) It is customary to start the left engine on a multi-engine aircraft first because the pilot can see and hear that engine better.

27. The recommended procedure for making tight turns during taxi operations is to use

    1. nosewheel steering.
    2. differential braking.
    3. differential power.
    4. nosewheel steering and differential braking.

28. _____ (True, False) It is a violation of FARs to begin a takeoff in a twin-engine airplane if the accelerate-stop distance is greater than the available runway and/or the existing airport density altitude is higher than the single-engine service ceiling.

29. If takeoff is initiated when the existing density altitude is higher than the single-engine service ceiling, an engine failure will result in a _____ _____.

30. _____ (True, False) The pilot of a twin-engine airplane taking off with less than accelerate-stop distance is no worse off than the pilot of a single-engine airplane under the same circumstances.

31. The safest procedure to follow when the accelerate-stop distance is longer than the available takeoff runway and the existing airport density altitude is higher than the single-engine service ceiling is to wait for more favorable winds and density altitude conditions and/or reduce gross weight by offloading _____, _____, or _____.

32. During the takeoff run, the pilot should check the r.p.m., MAP, and oil pressure/temperature in addition to checking the

    1. fuel-flow indicators and the airspeed indicator.
    2. exhaust gas temperature gauges and fuel selectors.
    3. flight instruments and the fuel quantity gauges.
    4. the flap position indicator and the cabin door.

33. After liftoff during a normal takeoff, the most desirable climb speed is

    1. between V_{XSE} and V_{YSE}.
    2. between V_{MC} and cruise climb speed.
    3. V_{YSE}.
    4. V_Y.

34. During a normal takeoff, the point of gear retraction should occur

    1. as soon as possible after liftoff.
    2. when a positive rate of climb has been established and insufficient runway remains for landing.
    3. as the airplane reaches a safe maneuvering altitude.
    4. just prior to the first power reduction.

35. List methods which are beneficial in reducing excessively hot cylinder head temperatures during climbout.

    1. _____
    2. _____
    3. _____
    4. _____
    5. _____

36. The most efficient and accurate method of adjusting the mixture at cruising altitude is through use of the

    1. EGT gauge.
    2. fuel-flow indicators.
    3. propeller synchronization system.
    4. power setting tables in the pilot's operating handbook.

37. Determine the number of nautical miles required to descend to the traffic pattern altitude under the following conditions.

    Cruising altitude . . . . 15,500 ft. MSL
    Traffic pattern altitude . . . . 1,500 ft. MSL
    Descent rate . . . . 700 f.p.m.
    Descent groundspeed . . . . 170 kts.

    1. 20 n.m.
    2. 37 n.m.
    3. 57 n.m.
    4. 63 n.m.

38. When should the prelanding checklist be completed?

    1. Prior to entering the traffic pattern
    2. Before turning base leg
    3. During base leg
    4. Anytime before short final approach

39. When should the propeller and mixture controls be placed in the full forward position during an approach?

    1. At traffic pattern entry
    2. During the prelanding check
    3. While turning from base leg to final
    4. Only when a go-around is imminent

40. _____ (True, False) A constant angle of descent is desirable during a short-field approach and landing.

41. _____ (True, False) It is seldom necessary to trim a multi-engine airplane during the performance of steep turns.

42. _____ (True, False) During practice of imminent stalls, an immediate, rapid power application should be made at the first indication of aerodynamic buffeting.

43. List the three basic indications of an imminent stall.

   1. _____
   2. _____
   3. _____

Exercise 1B –
General Systems

1. _____ (True, False) Propeller efficiency is determined mainly by the blade's angle of attack.

2. Aerodynamic forces acting on the blades of a spinning, constant speed propeller tend to twist the blades and _____ (increase, decrease) the angle of attack.

3. _____ (True, False) The propeller blade angle adjusts automatically to maintain a constant r.p.m. whenever a change in engine speed is sensed by the propeller governor.

4. The purpose of counterweights on a featherable propeller is to

   1. freeze the blade angle at the current setting in case of oil pressure loss.
   2. aid the propeller blades in moving towards high pitch.
   3. keep the propeller blades balanced during pitch changes.
   4. overcome the force of the compressed air in the feathering mechanism.

5. The two types of fuel pumps that provide fuel pressure to the engine are the _____-_____ and _____ _____ pumps.

6. _____ (True, False) Both types of fuel pumps should be checked prior to flight to insure that they are operating properly.

7. _____ (True, False) All fuel passes through the fuel selector valve enroute from the tank to the engine.

8. Generally, the crossfeed system is utilized during extended _____ _____-_____ operations.

9. _____ (True, False) Fuel strainers and tanks are the only locations in fuel systems where quick drain valves are located.

10. _____ (True, False) The engine-driven fuel pump of a fuel injection system should be run only during landings, takeoffs, or when switching fuel tanks.

11. _____ (True, False) A fuel-flow indicator can be used in leaning the fuel-air ratio.

12. _____ (True, False) As compared to carburetor systems, fuel injection systems are less susceptible to induction icing and allow the greatest amount of vaporization cooling at the cylinder head.

13. _____ (True, False) Either a manually controlled or automatic alternate air source normally is provided on an airplane with a fuel injection system.

14. _____ (True, False) The AC electrical power that the alternators produce is converted to DC power within the reverse current relay switch.

Match the basic electrical functions on the right with the associated system components on the left.

15. _____ Voltage regulator

16. _____ Bus bar

17. _____ Overvoltage light

18. _____ Overvoltage relay

19. _____ Alternator output circuit breaker

A. Indicates the respective alternator is off the line

B. Protects the electrical system if the output exceeds maximum voltage

C. Distributes power throughout the system

D. Maintains proper load sharing between alternators

E. Takes the alternator off the line in the event of excessive output

F. Protects the voltage regulators

20. A common power source for a retractable landing gear system is a

1. hydraulic hand pump.
2. vacuum-driven air pump.
3. one-way electric motor which drives a gearbox.
4. reversible electric motor which drives a hydraulic pump.

21. _____ (True, False) A blue radial line on the airspeed indicator marks the maximum speed for gear extension.

22. _____ (True, False) Most landing gear indicator lights can be checked for proper operation using a press-to-test feature.

23. If the gear is not down and locked when the throttle is reduced below an established power setting, the pilots of some light twins are warned by a _____ _____ _____.

24. _____ (True, False) Airspeed and pitch attitude are two flight characteristics which may provide an indication of a landing gear malfunction.

25. _____ (True, False) The turbocharger compressor is run by exhaust gases and delivers compressed air to the engine.

26. _____ (True, False) Maximum rated manifold pressure is available when operating above the turbocharger's critical altitude.

27. _____ (True, False) To prevent overboosting some turbocharged engines, a pressure relief valve opens when the manifold pressure produced by the compressor is too high.

28. Wing de-icing and anti-icing equipment on modern airplanes generally falls within the category of either _____ or _____.

29. _____ (True, False) Anti-icing equipment should be turned on prior to entering icing conditions or at the first indication of icing.

30. The two methods of heat origination used in cabin heating systems are _____ _____ _____ and _____ _____ _____.

CHAPTER 2—PERFORMANCE CONSIDERATIONS

Exercise 2A— Weight And Balance

Match the weight and balance terms on the left with the correct descriptions on the right.

1. _____ Maximum gross weight

2. _____ Basic empty weight

3. _____ Maximum landing weight

4. _____ Center of gravity

5. _____ Reference datum

6. _____ Moment

7. _____ Maximum takeoff weight

8. _____ Arm

A. Weight of an item multiplied by its arm

B. Distance between the datum reference and a specific item in the airplane

C. The point at which an airplane would balance if suspended

D. Maximum weight determined by the manufacturer for certification

E. An arbitrarily fixed position along the longitudinal axis of the airplane from which distances are measured for purposes of weight and balance computations

F. Maximum weight at which takeoff is permitted

G. Weight of a standard airplane including unusable fuel, full operating fluids, full oil, and optional equipment

H. Maximum weight allowed for landing

9. The moment of an item that weighs 240 pounds and is positioned 133 inches aft of the datum reference is _____ lb.-in.

10. The total weight of a loaded airplane is 3,200 pounds and the total moment is 320,000 lb.-in.; therefore, the CG is located _____ inches aft of the datum.

11. _____ (True, False) Since the effects of overstressing an airplane are cumulative, structural failure may be caused by occasionally exceeding the gross weight and load factor limitations.

12. The weight of 20 gallons of aviation fuel and eight quarts of engine oil is approximately _____ pounds.

13. If the CG exceeds the aft limit, as the airspeed is reduced during the landing approach, the elevator or stabilator loses effectiveness and the nose may pitch _____ (up, down) uncontrollably.

14. The location of the airplane's center of gravity is found by dividing the total moment by the total _____.

15. The moment for the weight placed in a particular aircraft compartment is calculated by multiplying the weight in pounds times its distance in inches from the airplane's
    1. mean aerodynamic chord.
    2. engine compartment.
    3. main landing gear.
    4. datum reference.

16. _____ (True, False) To determine CG location when using a 1,000-pound index, the total moment must be multiplied times 1,000 before it is divided by total weight.

17. _____ (True, False) The advantage of a moment index is that it reduces the size of the numbers in weight and balance computations.

18. An airplane with a CG location forward of limits will require a takeoff run which is _____ (longer, shorter) than normal.

19. What is the most dangerous condition for airplane weight and balance in terms of total weight and CG location?
    1. Over gross and CG forward of limits
    2. Over gross and CG aft of limits
    3. Under gross and CG forward of limits
    4. Under gross and CG aft of limits

Use the weight and moment tables, and the weight and balance form for a typical six-place airplane to answer questions 20 through 23.

SAMPLE WEIGHT AND BALANCE FORM

PAYLOAD COMPUTATIONS				REF	ITEM		WEIGHT	MOMENT/ 100
ITEM OCCUPANTS OR CARGO	ARM	WEIGHT	MOMENT/ 100	1.	BASIC EMPTY WEIGHT		3,472	1220.0
				2.	PAYLOAD			
Seat 1				3.	ZERO FUEL WEIGHT (sub-total) (Do not exceed maximum zero fuel weight)			
Seat 2								
Seat 3								
Seat 4				4.	FUEL LOADING	(main)		
Seat 5						(auxiliary)		
Seat 6						(wing lockers)		
BAGGAGE				5.	TAKEOFF WEIGHT			
PAYLOAD								
				6.	LESS FUEL TO DESTINATION	(main)		
						(auxiliary)		
						(wing lockers)		
				7.	LANDING WEIGHT			

WEIGHT AND MOMENT TABLES

BAGGAGE

WEIGHT (POUNDS)	NOSE COMPARTMENT ARM = -31"	WING LOCKER ARM = 63"	CABIN COMPARTMENTS		
			ARM = 96"	ARM = 124"	ARM = 126"
			MOMENT/100		
10	-3	6	10	12	13
20	-6	13	19	25	25
30	-9	19	29	37	38
40	-12	25	38	50	50
50	-16	32	48	62	63
60	-19	38	58	74	76
70	-22	44	67	87	88
80	-25	50	77	99	101
90	-28	57	86	112	113
100	-31	63	96	124	126
110	-34	69	106	136	139
120	-37	76	115	149	151
130	-40	82	125	161	164
140	-43	88	134	174	176
150	-46	94	144	186	189
160	-50	101	154	198	202
170	-53	107	163		
180	-56	113	173		
190	-59	120	182		
200	-62	126	192		
210	-65	132			
220	-68	139			
230	-71	145			
240	-74	151			
250	-78				
260	-81				
270	-84				
280	-87				
290	-90				
300	-93				
310	-96				
320	-99				
330	-102				
340	-105				
350	-108				

CREW AND PASSENGERS

WEIGHT (POUNDS)	1ST OR 2ND SEATS ARM = 37"	BENCH SEAT ARM = 71"	3RD OR 4TH SEATS INDIVIDUAL SEAT ARM = 68"	5TH OR 6TH SEAT ARM = 102"
			MOMENT/100	
10	4	7	7	10
20	7	14	14	20
30	11	21	20	31
40	15	28	27	41
50	18	36	34	51
60	22	43	41	61
70	26	50	48	71
80	30	57	54	82
90	33	64	61	92
100	37	71	68	102
110	41	78	75	112
120	44	85	82	122
130	48	92	88	133
140	52	99	95	143
150	56	106	102	153
160	59	114	109	163
170	63	121	116	173
180	67	128	122	184
190	70	135	129	194
200	74	142	136	204
210	78	149	143	214
220	81	156	150	224
230	85	163	156	235
240	89	170	163	245
250	92	178	170	255
260	96	185	177	265
270	100	192	184	275
280	104	199	190	286
290	107	206	197	296
300	111	213	204	306

FUEL

GALLONS	WEIGHT (POUNDS)	MAIN WING TANKS ARM = 35"	AUXILIARY WING TANKS ARM = 47"	WING LOCKER TANKS ARM = 49"
		MOMENT/100		
5	30	10	14	15
10	60	21	28	29
15	90	32	42	44
20	120	42	56	59
25	150	52	70	74
30	180	63	85	88
35	210	74	99	103
40	240	84	113	118
45	270	94	127	
50	300	105	141	
55	330	116	155	
60	360	126	169	
63	378	132	178	
65	390	136		
70	420	147		
75	450	158		
80	480	168		
85	510	178		
90	540	189		
95	570	200		
100	600	210		

20. Compute the takeoff weight and CG location under the following conditions.

Maximum takeoff weight	5,500 lbs.
Forward CG limit	32.0 in.
Aft CG limit	43.6 in.
Fuel loading	
Main	100 gals.
Auxiliary	63 gals.
Baggage (Station 126)	160 lbs.
Pilot (Seat 1)	180 lbs.
Passengers	
Seat 2	170 lbs.
Seat 3	130 lbs.
Seat 4	120 lbs.
Seat 5	110 lbs.
Seat 6	110 lbs.

The takeoff weight is _____ pounds and the CG is approximately _____ inches aft of the datum.

21. _____ (True, False) The airplane is within the CG limits for takeoff.

22. If the airplane burns a total of 85 gallons of fuel out of the main tanks and none out of the auxiliary tanks, what is the approximate CG for landing?

    1. 42.5 in.
    2. 43.0 in.
    3. 43.8 in.
    4. 44.1 in.

23. _____ (True, False) The airplane is within the CG limits for landing.

24. Assume an airplane is loaded out of CG limits and the pilot has determined some cargo must be moved from the aft compartment to the forward compartment. The following information is known.

    Gross weight . . . . 4,500 lbs.
    Forward CG limit . . . . 33.0 in.
    Aft CG limit . . . . 44.6 in.
    Forward compartment . . . . -10.0 in.
    Aft compartment . . . . 115.0 in.
    Aft cargo . . . . 135 lbs.
    Current CG . . . . 45.5 in.

    The minimum amount of weight that must be shifted to the forward compartment in order for the airplane to be within the CG limits is _____ pounds.

Exercise 2B– Performance Charts

When necessary, see the charts at the end of this exercise for solutions to appropriate questions.

1. Use the altitude conversion chart to determine density altitude under the following conditions.

   Pressure altitude . . . . 3,000 ft.
   Temperature . . . . 70° F

   Density altitude is _____ feet.

2. Use the flight computer to determine the density altitude under the listed conditions.

   Field elevation . . . . 6,100 ft.
   Altimeter setting 29.72
   Temperature . . . . 86° F

   The density altitude is

   1. 6,500 feet.
   2. 7,900 feet.
   3. 8,700 feet.
   4. 9,100 feet.

WORKBOOK EXERCISES

Match the operating conditions on the left with the corresponding effects on airplane performance on the right. Answers may be used more than once.

3. _____ Grass runway

4. _____ Uphill runway

5. _____ Hot day

6. _____ Light gross weight

7. _____ Low pressure altitude

A. Increased takeoff distance
B. Decreased landing distance
C. Decreased maximum rate of climb

Match the atmospheric conditions on the left with the probable effects on density altitude on the right. Answers may be used more than once.

8. _____ Outside temperature of 15° Celsius at a field elevation of 3,000 feet MSL

9. _____ Altimeter setting of 30.12 at a field elevation of 4,000 feet MSL (Assume standard temperature)

10. _____ Ground fog

11. _____ 10-knot headwind during takeoffs

A. Density altitude above true altitude
B. No effect on density altitude
C. Density altitude below true altitude

To answer questions 12 through 14, use the appropriate charts with the following conditions. Consider each question independently.

Temperature . . . . 25°C
Pressure altitude . . . . 2,000 ft.
Headwind component . . . . 23 m.p.h.
Gross weight . . . . 4,300 lbs.

12. The takeoff ground run for a short-field takeoff using 25° flaps is

1. 450 feet.
2. 550 feet.
3. 700 feet.
4. 900 feet.

13. The accelerate-stop distance with the flaps retracted is

    1. 2,100 feet.
    2. 2,410 feet.
    3. 2,470 feet.
    4. 2,530 feet.

14. The normal landing distance when landing over a 50-foot obstacle using 35° of flaps is

    1. 1,330 feet.
    2. 1,350 feet.
    3. 1,565 feet.
    4. 1,588 feet.

15. Determine the single-engine rate of climb from the appropriate chart using the listed conditions.

    Power setting . . . . Maximum continuous
    Flaps . . . . Retracted
    Gear . . . . Extended
    Propeller . . . . Feathered
    Temperature . . . . 40° F
    Standard altitude . . . . 8,000 ft.
    Gross weight . . . . 5,000 lbs.

    1. 335 f.p.m.
    2. 360 f.p.m.
    3. 535 f.p.m.
    4. 560 f.p.m.

16. Using the appropriate power setting tables, compute the manifold pressure, fuel flow, and true airspeed based on the following conditions.

    Power setting 65%
    Temperature . . . . +9°C
    Pressure altitude . . . . 13,000 ft.

    The manifold pressure is _____ in. Hg, the fuel flow is _____ g.p.h., and the true airspeed is _____ knots.

17. Determine the stalling speed in miles per hour for an airplane under the following conditions.

    Gross weight . . . . 3,900 lbs.
    Gear . . . . Extended
    Flaps . . . . Retracted

    1. 73 CAS
    2. 73 IAS
    3. 74 CAS
    4. 74 IAS

18. The values obtained from multi-engine airplane performance charts are based on

    1.   a safety factor of 10 percent.

    2.   average aircraft performance.

    3.   maximum performance of a new aircraft.

    4.   theoretical computations.

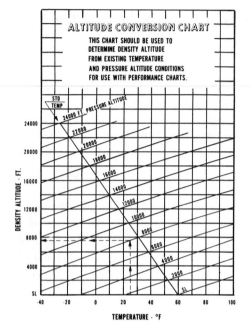

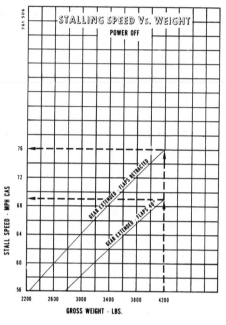

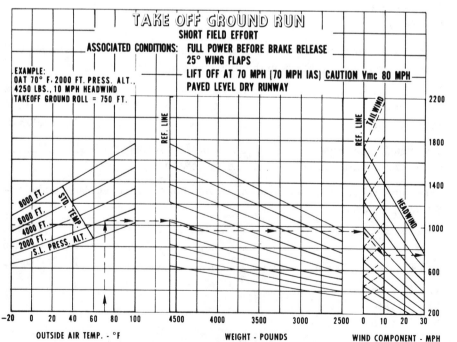

ACCELERATE STOP DISTANCE

CONDITIONS:
1. Power - FULL THROTTLE and 2700 RPM Before Brake Release.
2. Mixtures - LEAN for field elevation
3. Wing Flaps - UP.
4. Cowl Flaps - OPEN.
5. Level, Hard Surface, Dry Runway.
6. Engine Failure at Engine Failure Speed.
7. Idle Power and Heavy Braking After Engine Failure.

NOTE:
1. If full power is applied without brakes set, distances apply from point where full power is applied.
2. Decrease distance 3% for each 4 knots headwind.
3. Increase distance 5% for each 2 knots tailwind.

WEIGHT - POUNDS	ENGINE FAILURE SPEED - KIAS	PRESSURE ALTITUDE - FEET	TOTAL DISTANCE - FEET						
			-20°C -4°F	-10°C +14°F	0°C 32°F	+10°C +50°F	+20°C +68°F	+30°C +86°F	+40°C +104°F
5500	92	Sea Level	3020	3190	3370	3550	3740	3930	4120
		1000	3220	3400	3590	3790	3990	4210	4490
		2000	3430	3630	3830	4050	4340	4570	4820
		3000	3660	3880	4100	4400	4650	4910	5180
		4000	3920	4160	4480	4730	5000	5290	5590
		5000	4200	4530	4810	5090	5390	5700	6030
		6000	4590	4880	5180	5490	5820	6170	6530
		7000	4950	5270	5600	5940	6310	6700	7110
		8000	5360	5710	6070	6460	6870	7310	7780
		9000	5830	6210	6630	7060	7530	8020	8560
		10,000	6330	6770	7230	7720	8250	8810	9420
5100	88	Sea Level	2540	2680	2830	2980	3140	3300	3470
		1000	2710	2860	3020	3180	3350	3530	3710
		2000	2880	3050	3220	3390	3580	3770	3970
		3000	3070	3250	3440	3630	3830	4040	4330
		4000	3290	3480	3680	3900	4190	4420	4660
		5000	3520	3730	3950	4250	4500	4750	5020
		6000	3770	4010	4320	4580	4850	5130	5430
		7000	4060	4390	4660	4950	5240	5560	5890
		8000	4470	4750	5050	5360	5690	6050	6420
		9000	4840	5160	5490	5840	6220	6610	7030
		10,000	5250	5600	5970	6370	6790	7230	7710
4700	85	Sea Level	2110	2230	2350	2470	2600	2740	2870
		1000	2250	2370	2500	2640	2770	2920	3070
		2000	2390	2520	2660	2810	2960	3120	3280
		3000	2540	2690	2840	3000	3160	3340	3510
		4000	2720	2880	3040	3210	3390	3580	3780
		5000	2900	3080	3260	3440	3640	3840	4130
		6000	3110	3300	3500	3700	3910	4210	4450
		7000	3340	3550	3760	3990	4300	4550	4820
		8000	3600	3830	4070	4390	4660	4940	5230
		9000	3900	4230	4490	4770	5070	5380	5710
		10,000	4300	4580	4870	5180	5510	5860	6240
4300	81	Sea Level	1730	1820	1920	2020	2120	2230	2340
		1000	1830	1940	2040	2150	2260	2380	2500
		2000	1950	2060	2170	2290	2410	2530	2660
		3000	2070	2190	2310	2440	2570	2710	2850
		4000	2210	2340	2470	2610	2750	2900	3060
		5000	2360	2500	2640	2790	2950	3110	3280
		6000	2520	2680	2830	2990	3160	3340	3530
		7000	2710	2870	3040	3220	3410	3600	3880
		8000	2910	3090	3280	3470	3680	3970	4200
		9000	3140	3340	3550	3760	4070	4310	4570
		10,000	3390	3610	3830	4150	4410	4680	4970

NORMAL LANDING DISTANCE

CONDITIONS:
1. Throttles - IDLE.
2. Landing Gear - DOWN.
3. Wing Flaps - 35°.
4. Cowl Flaps - CLOSE.
5. Level, Hard Surface Runway.
6. Maximum Braking Effort.

NOTE:
1. Increase distance by 25% of ground run for operation on firm sod runway.
2. If necessary to land with wing flaps UP, the approach speed should be increased above the normal approach speed by 12 knots. Expect total landing distance to increase by 35%.
3. Decrease total distances by 3% for each 4 knots headwind. For operations with tailwinds up to 10 knots, increase total distances by 5% for each 2 knots wind.

WEIGHT-POUNDS	SPEED AT 50-FOOT OBSTACLE KIAS	PRESSURE ALTITUDE - FEET	20°C (68°F)		30°C (86°F)		40°C (104°F)	
			GROUND ROLL - FEET	TOTAL DISTANCE TO CLEAR 50-FOOT OBSTACLE	GROUND ROLL - FEET	TOTAL DISTANCE TO CLEAR 50-FOOT OBSTACLE	GROUND ROLL - FEET	TOTAL DISTANCE TO CLEAR 50-FOOT OBSTACLE
5400	93	Sea Level	660	1810	680	1830	700	1850
		1000	680	1830	700	1850	730	1880
		2000	710	1860	730	1880	750	1900
		3000	730	1880	760	1910	780	1930
		4000	760	1910	780	1930	810	1960
		5000	790	1940	810	1960	840	1990
		6000	820	1970	850	2000	870	2020
		7000	850	2000	880	2030	910	2060
		8000	880	2030	910	2060	940	2090
		9000	920	2070	950	2100	980	2130
		10,000	950	2100	980	2130	1020	2170
5000	89	Sea Level	550	1700	570	1720	590	1740
		1000	570	1720	590	1740	610	1760
		2000	600	1750	620	1770	640	1790
		3000	620	1770	640	1790	660	1810
		4000	640	1790	660	1810	680	1830
		5000	670	1820	690	1840	710	1860
		6000	690	1840	710	1860	740	1890
		7000	720	1870	740	1890	770	1920
		8000	750	1900	770	1920	800	1950
		9000	770	1920	800	1950	830	1980
		10,000	800	1950	830	1980	860	2010
4600	86	Sea Level	460	1610	480	1630	490	1640
		1000	480	1630	500	1650	510	1660
		2000	500	1650	510	1660	530	1680
		3000	520	1670	530	1680	550	1700
		4000	530	1680	550	1700	570	1720
		5000	550	1700	570	1720	590	1740
		6000	580	1730	600	1750	610	1760
		7000	600	1750	620	1770	640	1790
		8000	620	1770	640	1790	660	1810
		9000	650	1800	670	1820	690	1840
		10,000	670	1820	690	1840	720	1870
4200	82	Sea Level	380	1530	390	1540	410	1560
		1000	390	1540	410	1560	420	1570
		2000	410	1560	420	1570	440	1590
		3000	420	1570	440	1590	450	1600
		4000	440	1590	450	1600	470	1620
		5000	460	1610	470	1620	490	1640
		6000	470	1620	490	1640	500	1650
		7000	490	1640	510	1660	520	1670
		8000	510	1660	530	1680	540	1690
		9000	530	1680	550	1700	560	1710
		10,000	550	1700	570	1720	590	1740

WORKBOOK EXERCISES

SINGLE ENGINE CLIMB
STANDARD DAY (ISA)

ASSOCIATED CONDITIONS:

POWER	MAXIMUM CONTINUOUS
FLAPS	UP
GEAR	UP
CLIMB SPEED	IAS AS TABULATED
INOPERATIVE PROPELLER	FEATHERED

NOTE: DECREASE RATE-OF-CLIMB 25 FT/MIN FOR EACH 10°F ABOVE STANDARD DAY (ISA) TEMPERATURE.

WEIGHT POUNDS	CLIMB SPEED MPH ~ IAS
5990	122
5500	119
5000	116
4500	113

CONFIGURATION	APPROXIMATE RATE-OF-CLIMB LOSS ~ FT/MIN
GEAR DOWN	200
PROP WINDMILLING	200
GEAR DOWN AND PROP WINDMILLING	400

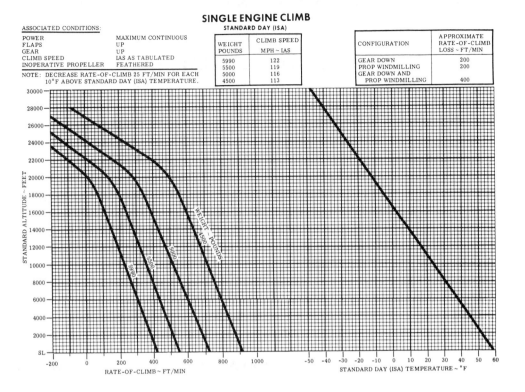

CRUISE POWER SETTINGS

65% MAXIMUM CONTINUOUS POWER (OR FULL THROTTLE)

PRESS ALT.	ISA-36°F (-20°C)							STANDARD DAY (ISA)							ISA +36°F (+20°C)						
	OAT	ENGINE SPEED	MAN. PRESS	FUEL FLOW PER ENGINE		TAS		OAT	ENGINE SPEED	MAN. PRESS	FUEL FLOW PER ENGINE		TAS		OAT	ENGINE SPEED	MAN. PRESS	FUEL FLOW PER ENGINE		TAS	
FEET	°C	RPM	IN HG	PPH	GPH	KTS	MPH	°C	RPM	IN HG	PPH	GPH	KTS	MPH	°C	RPM	IN HG	PPH	GPH	KTS	MPH
SL	-5	2500	28.9	112	18.6	173	199	15	2500	29.8	112	18.6	177	204	35	2500	30.6	112	18.6	180	207
2000	-9	2500	28.9	112	18.6	176	203	11	2500	29.8	112	18.6	180	207	31	2500	20.7	112	18.6	183	211
4000	-13	2500	29.0	112	18.6	179	206	7	2500	29.8	112	18.6	183	211	27	2500	30.9	112	18.6	186	214
6000	-17	2500	29.0	112	18.6	182	209	3	2500	29.9	112	18.6	186	214	23	2500	31.0	112	18.6	190	219
8000	-21	2500	29.2	112	18.6	185	213	-1	2500	30.0	112	18.6	189	218	19	2500	31.1	112	18.6	193	222
10000	-25	2500	29.2	112	18.6	188	216	-5	2500	30.2	112	18.6	193	222	15	2500	31.2	112	18.6	197	227
12000	-29	2500	29.2	112	18.6	192	221	-9	2500	30.3	112	18.6	196	226	11	2500	31.4	112	18.6	200	230
14000	-33	2500	29.2	112	18.6	195	224	-13	2500	30.4	112	18.6	200	230	7	2500	31.5	112	18.6	204	235
16000	-37	2500	29.3	112	18.6	199	229	-17	2500	30.5	112	18.6	204	235	3	2500	31.6	112	18.6	208	239
18000	-41	2500	29.3	112	18.6	202	233	-21	2500	30.6	112	18.6	207	238	-1	2500	31.7	112	18.6	212	244
20000	-44	2500	29.4	112	18.6	206	237	-24	2500	30.6	112	18.6	211	243	-4	2500	31.8	112	18.6	216	249
22000	-48	2500	29.5	112	18.6	211	243	-28	2500	30.8	112	18.6	216	249	-8	2500	32.0	112	18.6	221	254
24000	-53	2500	29.8	112	18.6	215	247	-33	2500	31.1	112	18.6	220	253	-13	2500	32.0	111	18.5	224	258
26000	-57	2500	30.0	112	18.6	219	252	-37	2500	31.3	112	18.6	225	259	-17	2500	32.0	109	18.2	227	261
28000	-61	2500	29.9	110	18.3	222	256	-41	2500	29.9	105	17.5	223	257	-21	2500	29.9	100	16.7	223	257
30000	-64	2500	26.4	94	15.7	210	242	-44	2500	26.4	91	15.1	210	242	-24	2500	26.4	88	14.7	206	237

CHAPTER 3—ENGINE-OUT OPERATIONS

Exercise 3A— Aerodynamics

1. _____ (True, False) According to FAR Part 23, a light twin-engine airplane weighing 5,500 pounds gross weight and having a V_{SO} of 58 knots is required to demonstrate a climb rate of at least 50 f.p.m. at 5,000 feet.

2. _____ (True, False) The left engine is the critical engine in all twin-engine airplanes.

3. _____ (True, False) Minimum control speed decreases as altitude increases.

4. _____ (True, False) Right engine failure in a conventional twin-engine airplane creates more control difficulties than failure of the left engine.

5. _____ (True, False) Lack of induced airflow after engine failure will cause the airplane to roll in the direction of the inoperative engine.

6. If an engine-out climb is not possible, the slowest rate of descent can be attained by using the single engine best _____-of-climb airspeed.

7. If an engine-out climb is not possible, it is because
   1. lift exceeds drag.
   2. drag exceeds thrust.
   3. thrust is greater than lift.
   4. drag and lift are equal.

8. The slowest speed at which the control surfaces can overcome the turning tendency caused by asymmetrical thrust is called
   1. V_{SO}.
   2. V_2.
   3. V_{MC}.
   4. V_{NE}.

9. The least amount of drag is created when the propeller of the inoperative engine is
   1. windmilling.
   2. feathered.
   3. stopped with a low blade angle.
   4. stopped with a high blade angle.

10. In high angle-of-attack attitudes, the descending blade of the propeller is asymmetrically loaded because

    1. it produces more thrust than the ascending blade.
    2. it is heavier than the ascending blade.
    3. the propeller has three blades.
    4. the ascending blade creates more effective torque.

Match the choice on the right with the corresponding term on the left.

11. _____ Single-engine service ceiling

12. _____ Single-engine absolute ceiling

13. _____ Induced drag

14. _____ Critical engine

15. _____ Minimum control speed

16. _____ Single-engine best rate-of-climb

17. _____ Greatest parasite drag

A. Caused by a windmilling propeller

B. That engine whose failure most adversely affects performance

C. Maximum density altitude at which V_{YSE} produces a 50 f.p.m. rate of climb

D. That airspeed below which directional control cannot be maintained with one engine out and the other developing takeoff power

E. Maximum density altitude the airplane is capable of attaining or maintaining

F. Airspeed that produces the least rate of descent with the operating engine at maximum continuous power

G. Caused by control surface deflection

18. List, in order, the factors which create the greatest amount of drag during an engine-out situation in most twin-engine airplanes.

    1. _____
    2. _____
    3. _____
    4. _____

A. Control responses necessary to counteract asymmetrical thrust and drag
B. Extension of the landing gear
C. Extension of full flaps
D. Windmilling propeller

Exercise 3B–
Procedures And Maneuvers

1. _____ (True, False) If an engine is producing only partial power, it should be considered a failed engine and shut down immediately.

2. Immediately following an engine failure, the pilot's primary concern is to
   1. identify the inoperative engine.
   2. feather the propeller.
   3. maintain aircraft control.
   4. apply maximum power.

3. The first indication of an engine failure is a pronounced yaw towards the _____ (operative, inoperative) engine.

4. _____ (True, False) To verify that the failed engine has been identified correctly, the pilot should place the appropriate mixture control in the idle cutoff position.

5. If an engine failure occurs during the takeoff ground run before the single-engine minimum control speed is reached, the pilot should
   1. accelerate the airplane to V_{XSE} on the ground and continue the takeoff.
   2. place both mixtures in idle cutoff and apply full flaps for aerodynamic braking.
   3. feather both propellers and apply the brakes, if necessary.
   4. discontinue the takeoff by closing both throttles and apply heavy braking, if required.

6. If an engine-out climb is not possible, the slowest rate of descent can be attained by using the single-engine best _____-of-climb airspeed.

7. When one engine is inoperative, the primary aerodynamic control used to overcome yaw is the _____.

8. _____ (True, False) During an engine-out approach to a landing, a higher-than-normal approach speed is maintained.

9. _____ (True, False) If an engine failure occurs during climb, the use of V_{XSE} will produce a greater rate of climb than that produced by V_{YSE}.

10. _____ (True, False) During an engine-out approach, the wing flaps should be used as little as possible, preferably not at all until the landing is assured.

11. The two most critical phases of flight in a multi-engine airplane are
    _____ and _____.

12. _____ (True, False) During the climb immediately following liftoff,
    attaining airspeed in excess of the multi-engine best rate-of-climb speed is not as
    valuable as gaining altitude.

13. If an engine failure occurs at the multi-engine service ceiling, the pilot may
    expect the airplane to drift down to the single-engine _____ ceiling.

14. The most frequent cause of an enroute engine failure is

    1. an internal mechanical failure.
    2. an ignition failure.
    3. a lubrication malfunction.
    4. interrupted fuel flow.

15. If an engine fails while enroute, the alternate airport which is selected should be
    the closest in terms of _____.

16. During the takeoff, the most critical point for an engine failure to occur is

    1. prior to reaching V_{MC}.
    2. between V_{MC} and V_{YSE}.
    3. between V_{YSE} and V_Y.
    4. after reaching V_{XSE} but before reaching obstacle clearance altitude.

17. Assume an engine-out landing approach is being performed with the right engine
    inoperative and the airplane trimmed for straight flight. When the left throttle is
    closed during the landing flare, pressure will be required on the _____
    (right, left) rudder pedal.

18. _____ (True, False) During an engine-out approach to landing, a
    higher-than-normal approach angle is maintained on final approach.

19. List three methods of identifying an inoperative engine.

    1. _____
    2. _____
    3. _____

20. List, in sequence, the power settings which should be applied immediately
    following an engine failure.

    1. _____
    2. _____
    3. _____

PILOT BRIEFINGS

INTRODUCTION

Pilot briefings are a series of essay-type questions designed to provoke further study and discussion of training concepts. Each briefing is assigned at a strategic point in the training syllabus. Prior to the briefing session, the applicant should complete the appropriate exercise by writing the answer to each question on a separate sheet of paper. During the briefing, the applicant and instructor will review each question and answer, then discuss related information. Answers to most of the pilot briefing questions are found in the textbook, while others may be found in the pilot's operating handbook or other appropriate publication.

MULTI-ENGINE OPERATIONS AND SYSTEMS
PROCEDURES AND MANEUVERS

1. Explain the elements contributing to the left-turning tendency in a conventional twin with both engines operating.

2. Explain the uses of differential power during taxi and takeoff.

3. Why are the effects of torque eliminated in airplanes with counter-rotating propellers?

4. How is asymmetrical loading of the propeller affected by angle of attack?

5. What factors limit the operating altitudes of light twin-engine airplanes?

6. Explain the difference between V_X and V_Y.

7. How is power affected by altitude, for both normally aspirated and turbocharged engines?

8. Why does torque cause a rolling moment in conventional twin-engine airplanes?

9. Why does loss of induced airflow cause a loss of total lift?

10. Begin with the slowest V-speed that is shown on the airspeed indicator and describe each speed in order, including its significance.

11. Describe the preflight planning considerations necessary for a typical multi-engine cross-country flight.

12. Describe the important aspects of takeoff planning.

13. Should a takeoff be initiated when the accelerate-stop distance under existing conditions exceeds the length of the available runway?

14. Should a takeoff be initiated when the existing airport density altitude is higher than the single-engine service ceiling?

15. Describe the correct procedures and sequence of events for a normal takeoff.

16. Explain the correct procedures and sequence of events for performing a short-field takeoff over obstacles.

17. How does published V_{MC} affect the rotation point during a normal takeoff?

18. What guidelines normally determine the point of gear retraction following liftoff?

19. When is the first power reduction normally made during departure?

20. Which is more valuable during initial climb, airspeed in excess of V_Y or altitude? Why?

21. What determines the configuration of the cowl flaps during a climb?

22. What are the advantages of performing a cruise climb to altitude?

23. Assuming full fuel tanks at departure, what is the sequence of fuel management throughout a cross-country flight?

24. Explain the factors involved in planning the descent to the destination airport.

25. Explain the correct procedures and sequence of events for a normal approach and landing.

26. Explain the correct procedures and sequence of events for a short-field landing over an obstacle.

27. During a short-field landing, what speed is used on the final approach? How does this speed compare with the single-engine minimum control speed?

28. Describe the correct procedures for performing a go-around from short final approach.

29. Explain the procedure for establishing flight at minimum controllable airspeed. What determines whether or not the aircraft is at minimum controllable airspeed?

30. Explain the procedures for setting up and executing imminent stalls in the approach-to-landing and take-off-and-departure configurations.

GENERAL SYSTEMS

1. Explain how a constant speed propeller operates on a multi-engine airplane.

2. Explain how to use the propeller control lever.

3. What happens when the propeller control lever is moved to the full aft position?

4. What are the maximum continuous operating power settings for the training airplane? Why is it important to comply with these limitations?

5. Explain the procedures involved with power application or reduction.

6. Explain the propeller synchronizing system.

7. Is an autofeather system installed on the training airplane? If so, explain how the system works.

8. How does a reversible propeller system work? Can it be used in flight?

9. Diagram and explain the fuel system used in the training airplane.

10. Explain the type of pumps available to provide fuel pressure to the engines.

11. Explain the operation of the fuel selector control.

12. Explain the crossfeed system on the training airplane. When is it generally used?

13. For what purpose are fuel tank vents installed?

14. What is the purpose of fuel strainers, or gascolators?

15. Where are the quick drains located?

16. What is the normal fuel pressure and what are some of the things that will cause low pressure?

17. Explain the fuel injection system.

18. Explain the primary sources of electrical power.

19. What is the function of a voltage regulator?

20. Explain the purpose of an over-voltage relay.

21. How is electrical power distributed through the airplane?

22. Explain what adjustments have to be made with one alternator inoperative.

23. Explain the landing gear system used on the training airplane.

24. Explain the safety features designed into the landing gear system.

25. How is emergency landing gear extension accomplished?

26. Explain turbocharging and the operational characteristics of this type of system.

27. Explain the following ice control systems, if installed on the training airplane.

    1. Propeller
    2. Wing and tail surfaces
    3. Windshield

28. What type of cabin heating system is installed on the training airplane?

29. Explain how the cabin heating system operates.

30. How is the temperature in the cabin regulated?

PERFORMANCE CONSIDERATIONS

WEIGHT AND BALANCE

1. For the training airplane, what are the maximum gross, maximum takeoff, maximum landing, and basic empty weights?

2. Which weights are required for gross weight computations?

3. Where is the basic empty weight found?

4. Which items are included in the payload?

5. What guidelines are used for making weight and balance computations if the weights of the passengers are unknown?

6. What is zero fuel weight?

7. Does the training airplane have a maximum zero fuel weight?

8. What is the purpose of a maximum zero fuel weight?

9. How does exceeding weight limits affect airplane performance?

10. Which item is used most often to adjust gross weight within limits when the plane has been overloaded?

11. Explain the following terms.
    1. Center of gravity
    2. Reference datum
    3. Arm
    4. Moment

12. What are three methods used to determine the center of gravity of an airplane?

13. Which method is used for the training airplane?

14. If the airplane is loaded to maximum capacity, will the greatest movement in center of gravity occur when weight is shifted from the fuel, baggage, or passenger loading station?

15. Assuming the listed conditions, determine whether the airplane is loaded within the center of gravity range.

    Pilot and front passenger. . .340 lbs.
    Rear passengers . . . . . 370 lbs.
    Fuel tanks . . . . Full
    Baggage . . . . .95 lbs.

16. Assuming that the airplane is loaded with the CG at the extreme aft limit, explain the handling characteristics of the airplane during normal operations, such as takeoffs and landings.

PERFORMANCE CHARTS

1. Given the following conditions, determine the accelerate-stop distance, the normal takeoff ground run, and the takeoff distance necessary to clear a 50-foot obstacle.

   Field elevation . . . . . 2,000 ft.
   Temperature . . . . 87°F
   Altimeter setting 29.72
   Runway . . . . . . Hard surfaced
   Weight . . . . . Maximum gross
   Headwind component . . 10 m.p.h.

2. Assuming the airplane is loaded to maximum gross weight, compute the average rate of climb between the pressure altitudes of 5,000 and 10,000 feet if the temperature is 60° F at both altitudes.

3. Determine the calibrated and indicated stalling speeds under the following conditions.

    Angle of bank . . . . 50°
    Gear . . . . Extended
    Flaps . . . . Retracted

4. Given the following conditions, determine the normal landing roll and the landing distance over a 50-foot obstacle.

    Field elevation . . . . . 3,500 ft.
    Temperature . . . . 82° F
    Altimeter setting 30.32
    Weight . . . . . . Maximum gross

5. Determine the power settings that will provide 65 percent rated horsepower under the following conditions.

    Pressure altitude . . . . 7,000 ft.
    Temperature . . . . 64° F

6. What are the single-engine minimum control speed and single-engine absolute ceiling for the training airplane? What is the significance of each of these values?

ENGINE-OUT OPERATIONS

AERODYNAMICS

1. Define critical engine.

2. Does partial power loss affect V_{MC}? Why? Does altitude affect V_{MC}? Why?

3. Explain why airplanes with counter-terrotating propellers do not have a critical engine.

4. Why is the airplane directionally uncontrollable during flight below V_{MC}?

5. Why should the propeller of the inoperative engine be feathered if it cannot be restarted immediately?

6. How does asymmetrical loading of the propeller affect directional stability during single-engine operation?

7. Identify and explain all the factors that contribute to the rolling tendency of the airplane in the direction of the inoperative engine.

8. Explain why some airplanes may not be able to maintain altitude after engine failure.

9. Explain how loading and balance can affect V_{MC}.

10. Why does a 50 percent reduction of power cause an approximate 80 percent decrease in climb performance?

11. How is performance affected during an attempt to restart a failed engine with the propeller feathered?

12. Explain the operational significance of the single-engine service ceiling and the single-engine absolute ceiling.

13. How are V_{YSE} and V_{XSE} related to single-engine ceilings?

14. What guidelines should be followed when making turns with one engine inoperative?

15. Explain the relative order of drag factors during engine-out operations as they apply to the training airplane.

16. In terms of single-engine operation, what are the advantages of reducing operating gross weights?

17. Explain the effect of a turn on the production of induced drag.

18. What are the relative advantages of multi-engine airplanes equipped with counterrotating propellers compared to conventional twins in terms of engine-out operations and performance?

19. Explain the relationship between excess thrust available and total drag as they relate to engine-out climbs.

20. Why is configuration so important during engine-out operations?

PROCEDURES AND MANEUVERS

1. Discuss the effects of banking the airplane toward the operative engine during single-engine flight.

2. What factors should be considered before shutting down an engine and feathering the propeller?

3. Explain why the takeoff and climb are considered to be the most critical phases of flight.

4. What procedure is used to regain airplane control if an engine failure occurs during flight below V_{MC}?

5. What indications does the pilot have that the airplane is approaching V_{MC}?

6. Is a successful engine-out go-around probable from a low altitude when the airspeed is below V_{YSE}?

7. Describe the use of the landing gear and wing flaps during an engine-out approach and landing.

8. In the event an engine failure occurs enroute, is the distance or time required to reach the alternate airport the most important consideration? Why?

9. If the right engine fails, which rudder will be required to counteract yaw?

10. Explain why rudder, rather than aileron, should be used to counteract the effects of asymmetrical thrust.

11. Describe, in sequence, the items on the single-engine emergency checklist that should be committed to memory.

12. Why is the throttle of the suspected inoperative engine retarded prior to beginning the feathering procedure?

13. Define accelerate-stop distance and explain why it is an important performance consideration.

14. When considering an engine failure, which is more valuable, airspeed in excess of V_{YSE} or additional altitude? Why?

15. Does the shutdown of either engine affect the operation of the landing gear, flaps, hydraulic system, or electrical system?

16. If a positive engine-out rate of climb is not possible, how is the minimum rate of descent obtained?

17. What procedure should be followed if an engine develops low oil pressure, but the flight is close to the destination airport?

18. Is an engine shutdown recommended if low oil pressure, but normal temperature is observed?

19. Explain the steps necessary to secure the engine after complete engine shutdown.

20. Is it possible for the airplane to enter a single-engine stall before V_{MC} is reached?

21. Why is it important to plan for an engine failure prior to initiating a takeoff?

MULTI-ENGINE FLIGHT TEST
ORAL EXAM

1. What documents are required to be onboard the airplane during flight operations? Explain the significance of each.

2. When is the next annual, 100-hour, or programmed maintenance inspection due?

3. Begin with the slowest V-speed shown on the airspeed indicator and describe each speed in order, including its significance.

4. Based upon the following data, determine the CG location.

   Pilot and front passenger. . .350 lbs.
   Center passengers. . . . . . 335 lbs.
   Fuel tanks . . . . Full
   Baggage. . . . . .75 lbs.

5. Use the weight and balance data from the previous question and assume that when an intermediate stop is made, the airplane has consumed 28 gallons of fuel and a 150-pound center seat passenger deplanes. How many inches will the center of gravity move and in which direction?

6. What grade and type of fuel and oil are specified for the airplane? How is the fuel checked to be certain the airplane has been serviced with the proper grade?

7. How is fuel contamination avoided during and after servicing?

8. Determine the amount of oxygen required for a flight at 15,000 feet for two hours with a total of three people onboard. How is the oxygen system checked and serviced?

9. Define the term *critical engine*. What determines the critical engine?

10. Define accelerate-stop distance and its significance.

11. Determine the accelerate-stop distance under the following conditions.

    Field pressure altitude . . 2,500 ft.
    Temperature . . . . 52°F
    Headwind component . 10 m.p.h.
    Weight . . . . Maximum gross

12. Compute the takeoff distance over a 50-foot obstacle based on the following data.

    Field elevation . . . . 3,000 ft.
    Altimeter setting 30.20
    Temperature . . . . 68°F
    Headwind component . . 15 m.p.h.
    Weight . . . . . . Maximum gross

13. Using the data from the previous question, determine the takeoff distance with no obstacles.

14. What power setting will produce 65 percent rated power at 7,000 feet if the temperature is 34°F?

15. Based on the information from the previous question, determine the true airspeed and maximum range if the airplane is loaded to gross weight.

16. How does gross weight affect the stalling speed of the airplane?

17. Determine the stalling speed differential between the following configurations.

    Power . . . . Off
    Gear . . . . Extended
    Flaps . . . . Retracted
    Weight . . . . Maximum gross
    Bank angle . . . . 55°

    Power . . . . Off
    Gear . . . . Extended
    Flaps . . . . Extended
    Weight . . . . Maximum gross
    Bank angle . . . . 35°

18. Compute the average multi-engine rate of climb between the altitudes of 5,000 and 10,000 feet MSL under the listed conditions.

    Altimeter 30.17
    Temperature at 5,000 feet . 31°F
    Temperature at 10,000 feet . 0°F
    Weight . . . . Maximum gross
    Airspeed . . . . . Best rate of climb

19. Based on the previous question, what indicated airspeed should be used to initially achieve the best rate of climb?

20. Given the following conditions, determine the average single-engine rate of climb between sea level and 2,000 feet MSL.

    Altimeter 29.92
    Temperature at sea level . . 77°F
    Temperature at 2,000 feet . 70°F
    Weight . . . . . . Maximum gross

21. Explain how the best single-engine rate-of-climb and best single-engine angle-of-climb airspeeds change with an increase in altitude.

22. What is the single-engine service ceiling for the training airplane and what is its significance in relation to takeoffs and go-arounds?

23. Explain the relationship between density altitude and the single-engine service ceiling.

24. Given the following data, determine the landing distance required over a 50-foot obstacle.

    Field pressure altitude . . 1,500 ft.
    Temperature . . . . 80°F
    Weight . . . . . Maximum landing
    Headwind . . . . 15 m.p.h.

25. Determine the landing ground roll given the following conditions.

    Field elevation . . . . 500 ft.
    Altimeter setting 29.29
    Temperature . . . . 65°F
    Weight . . . . . Maximum landing
    Headwind 0

26. What is the correct takeoff and landing technique during operations on a runway that has an accumulation of snow or mud?

27. Explain the technique of using asymmetrical power during cross-wind taxi.

28. Explain the electrical system installed in the training airplane.

29. During single-engine operations, are there any restrictions and/or recommendations placed on the electrical system operation?

30. Discuss the hot starting procedure for the training airplane and explain how the pilot can determine when this procedure is necessary.

31. Explain the procedure for correcting an engine overheating problem.

32. Explain the correct and most accurate engine leaning procedures.

33. Explain and diagram the airplane's fuel system.

34. Discuss the proper procedure for fuel management for both twin-engine and single-engine operations.

35. Are there any restrictions placed on the airplane with regard to minimum fuel for operation?

36. What is the danger of operating an airplane with a leaking fuel strainer?

37. What is the procedure if an engine failure occurs below V_{MC} on the takeoff ground run?

38. Under what circumstances may it be inadvisable to feather a propeller?

39. Once the propeller control is placed in the feathered position, approximately how many seconds are required for the propeller to feather?

40. List four methods of determining the inoperative engine.

41. Can the manifold pressure gauge and/or the tachometer indication be a reliable clue to which engine has failed?

42. Explain the propeller feathering procedures.

43. Is there any engine r.p.m. limitation on propeller feathering?

44. Explain the in-flight engine restart procedure if a propeller is feathered.

45. Explain why it is advisable to bank the airplane five degrees toward the operating engine during single-engine operations.

46. During single-engine operations, what is the slowest airspeed that is considered to be safe?

47. What gear/flap configurations and conditions were used to determine the published single-engine minimum control speed?

48. What is the proper recovery method if the pilot inadvertently allows the speed to dissipate to the single-engine minimum control speed during single-engine operations?

49. In the training airplane, is the greatest amount of drag created by the extension of the landing gear, extension of full flaps, or a windmilling propeller?

50. Explain the correct drag cleanup procedure for a go-around following a full flap approach to a landing.

51. How does landing gear extension affect the single-engine minimum control speed?

52. Is the landing gear electric, hydraulic, or a combination of the two?

53. How many seconds are required for the landing gear to retract fully? In what situation could this become critical?

54. Is it recommended for the pilot to make a definite effort to neutralize the rudder pressure prior to the landing gear retraction cycle?

55. What is the purpose of the landing gear safety switch and where is it located?

56. Which is the more critical situation—inability to extend or retract the landing gear normally?

57. Explain the landing procedure and configuration if the nosewheel will not extend and the two main wheels extend normally.

58. Explain the manual landing gear extension procedure.

59. What action should be taken in the event the propeller de-icing equipment fails on one prop?

60. If the airplane is autopilot equipped, is there any limitation placed on autopilot operation during single-engine flight?

61. What type of installation provides heated air to the cabin? Is there any limitation or restriction on this unit's operation?

62. Where is the alternate static source located and how is it put into operation?

WORKBOOK ANSWERS

EXERCISE 1A—PROCEDURES AND MANEUVERS

1. True
2. False
3. 3
4. 2
5. False
6. absolute ceiling
7. False
8. D
9. A
10. B
11. E
12. C
13. K
14. I
15. L
16. J
17. G
18. H
19. F
20. E
21. B
22. A
23. C
24. D
25. False

26. False
27. 3
28. False
29. forced landing
30. True
31. fuel, baggage, passengers
32. 1
33. 4
34. 2
35. 1. Level off momentarily
    2. Open cowl flaps
    3. Enrich mixture
    4. Increase engine r.p.m.
    5. Use a higher climb speed
36. 1
37. 3
38. 2
39. 2
40. True
41. False
42. False
43. 1. Reduction in sound level
    2. Decreasing control response
    3. Aerodynamic buffeting

EXERCISE 1B—GENERAL SYSTEMS

1. True
2. decrease
3. True
4. 2
5. engine-driven, electric boost
6. True
7. True
8. emergency single-engine
9. False
10. False
11. True
12. True
13. True
14. False
15. D
16. C

17. A
18. B
19. E
20. 4
21. False
22. True
23. gear warning horn
24. True
25. True
26. False
27. True
28. pneumatic, electric
29. True
30. gasoline combustion heaters, manifold heat exchangers

EXERCISE 2A—WEIGHT AND BALANCE

1. D
2. G
3. H
4. C
5. E
6. A
7. F
8. B
9. 31,920
10. 100
11. True
12. 135

13. up
14. weight
15. 4
16. True
17. True
18. longer
19. 2
20. 5430, 43
21. True
22. 3
23. False
24. 32.4

EXERCISE 2B—PERFORMANCE CHARTS

1. 4,200
2. 4
3. A
4. A, B
5. A, C
6. B
7. A, C
8. A
9. C

10. B
11. B
12. 2
13. 1
14. 2
15. 1
16. 31.45, 37.2, 202
17. 1
18. 3

EXERCISE 3A—AERODYNAMICS

1. False
2. False
3. True
4. False
5. True
6. rate
7. 2
8. 3
9. 2
10. 1
11. C

12. E
13. G
14. B
15. D
16. F
17. A
18. 1. D
    2. C
    3. B
    4. A

EXERCISE 3B—PROCEDURES AND MANEUVERS

1. False
2. 3
3. inoperative
4. False
5. 4
6. rate
7. rudder
8. False
9. False
10. True
11. takeoff, climb
12. True

13. absolute
14. 4
15. time
16. 2
17. right
18. False
19. 1. Direction of yaw
    2. "Idle foot, idle engine" test
    3. The engine instruments
20. 1. Mixtures—rich
    2. Propeller controls—high r.p.m.
    3. Throttles—maximum power

ALPHABETICAL INDEX

ALPHABETICAL INDEX

Pages Changes

1-80,   "The practice of entering this maneuver by increasing pitch attitude
1-81   to a high point with both engines operating and then reducing power
(Cont'd) on the critical engine should be avoided because the airplane may
         become uncontrollable when power on the critical engine is reduced.

"To conserve altitude during the engine inoperative loss of directional
control demonstration, recovery should be made by reducing the angle
of attack and resuming controlled flight. If a situation exists where
reduction of power on the operating engine is necessary to maintain
airplane control, the decision to reduce power must be made by the
pilot to avoid uncontrolled flight. Emphasis should be placed on con-
servation of altitude but not at the expense of uncontrolled flight.

"Recoveries should never be made by increasing power on the simulated failed engine."

In all V_{MC} demonstrations, *recovery should be started promptly at
the first indication of a stall or loss of directional control.*

NOTE: Multi-engine applicants should seek the advice of a qualified flight
instructor early in their training and review the appropriate PTS for terminology changes, additional guidelines, or caution notes. The new private PTS
includes specific objectives for all of the required tasks. For example, stalls,
maneuvering at minimum controllable airspeed, turn maneuvers, and maneuvering with one engine inoperative list an objective of 3,000 feet above
ground level as the minimum recovery altitude. In addition, a private pilot
with airplane single-engine land and instrument ratings who wants to add an
airplane multi-engine land rating, must demonstrate competency in all tasks
listed under the instrument flight portion of the PTS. One of those tasks is to
demonstrate competency in instrument approaches with one engine
inoperative. If the applicant decides not to demonstrate competency in instrument flight, the applicant's multi-engine privileges will be limited to VFR
operations only.

TEXTUAL UPDATE INFORMATION

New *Private Pilot Practical Test Standards* (PTS) supersede the advisory circular flight test guide for private pilots on August 31, 1985. The PTS contain several changes which concern applicants for the multi-engine rating. Specific guidelines or safety precautions apply to certain maneuvers, and numerous terminology changes are included. The following list identifies the affected pages in the *Multi-Engine Pilot Manual* and the PTS changes that apply to these pages. In addition, pages 1-66, 1-68, and 1-69 should be updated as indicated.

Pages   Changes

1-11   Lift-off speed for the short-field takeoff should indicate V_X, V_{MC} + 5 knots, or the recommended airspeed, whichever is greater.

1-15   Steep power turns now are referred to as "constant-altitude turns."

1-15,   Approach-to-landing stalls now are called "stalls, gear down and
1-16   approach flaps" or "stalls, gear down and full flaps." Takeoff and departure stalls now are called "stalls, gear up and flaps up."

1-17   Accelerated maneuver stalls are not required in the new private pilot PTS.

1-66, V_{MC} is not necessarily determined at gross weight. FAR Part 23
1-68   specifies: "The maximum sea level takeoff weight (or any lesser weight necessary to show V_{MC})."

1-69   The first paragraph should read ". . . the actual V_{MC} will be lower if the airplane CG is forward of the aft limit. Conversely, the V_{MC} will be higher if the airplane CG is at the aft limit." Increased weight, by itself, does not increase V_{MC}.

1-80,   The V_{MC} demonstration is called an "engine inoperative loss of direc-
1-81   tional control demonstration" in the new PTS and the following guidelines and/or caution notes are included:

"There is a density altitude above which the stalling speed is higher than the engine inoperative minimum control speed. When this density altitude exists close to the ground because of high elevations and/or high temperatures, an effective flight demonstration of loss of directional control may be hazardous and should not be attempted. If it is determined prior to flight that the stall speed is higher than V_{MC} and this flight demonstration is impractical, the significance of the engine inoperative minimum control speed may be emphasized by oral questioning, including the results of attempting engine inoperative flight below this speed, the recognition of loss of directional control, and proper recovery techniques.